CLASSIC WARPLANES

MESSERSCHMITT
Bf 109
Alfred Price

SMITHMARK

A SALAMANDER BOOK

©Salamander Books Ltd. 1992
129-137 York Way,
London N7 9LG,
United Kingdom.

ISBN 0-8317-1419-0

This edition published in 1992 by
SMITHMARK Publishers, Inc., 112
Madison Avenue, New York, NY 10016.

SMITHMARK Books are available for
bulk purchase for sales promotion and
premium use. For details write or
telephone the Manager of Special Sales,
SMITHMARK Publishers, Inc., 112
Madison Avenue, New York, NY 10016.
(212) 532-6660.

All correspondence concerning the
content of this volume should be
addressed to Salamander Books Ltd.

This book may not be sold outside the
United States of America or Canada.

CREDITS

Editor: Chris Westhorp
Designer: Tony Jones
Color Artwork: ©Pilot Press Ltd.
Three-view, side-view and cutaway
drawings: ©Pilot Press Ltd, England.
Filmset by: The Old Mill, England.
Color reproduction by Graham Curtis
Repro, England.
Printed in Belgium by Proost International
Book Production, Turnhout.

AUTHOR

ALFRED PRICE served in the Royal Air Force as an aircrew officer and, in the course of a flying career spanning 15 years, logged some 4,000 flying hours. In 1974 he left the RAF to become a full-time writer on aviation and related subjects. To date he has written 35 books and co-authored four more. These include "The Hardest Day" and "Battle of Britain Day" on the Battle of Britain, "Target Berlin" on the U.S. daylight air offensive on Germany, "One Day in a Long War" on the air war over North Vietnam and "Air War South Atlantic" on the air actions of the Falklands conflict. He holds a Ph.D in History from Loughborough University and is a Fellow of the Royal Historical Society.

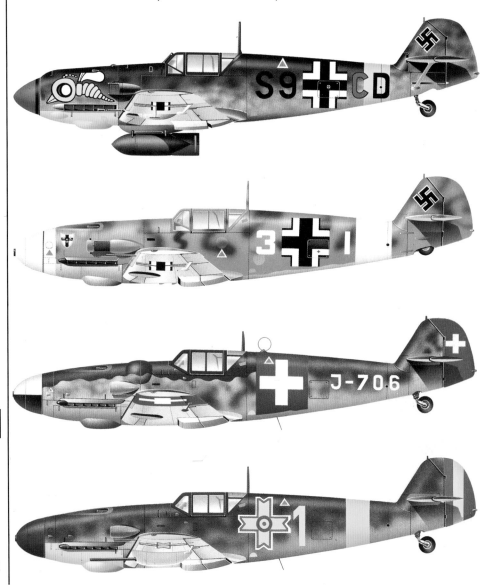

CONTENTS

HISTORY AND DEVELOPMENT 6

COMBAT 12

DEVELOPING THE BREED FURTHER 26

FOREIGN AND POST WAR SERVICE 42

INDEX 46

The mid-1930s was a period of rapid and far-reaching technical change in the field of aviation which spawned a generation of aircraft different in shape and far superior in capability to the fabric-covered, fixed-undercarriage biplanes that had gone before them.

In the Summer of 1934 the German Air Ministry issued a requirement for a single-seat monoplane interceptor fighter to replace the Heinkel He 51 and Arado Ar 68 biplanes then in service. Willy Messerschmitt, a gifted young designer with no reputation to lose and possibly one to gain, eagerly accepted the challenge and sought to push the state of the art as far as it would go. He did not stint himself. His new fighter incorporated almost every innovation then possible: it was a streamlined airframe of all-metal stressed skin construction, with a retractable undercarriage, enclosed cockpit and a thin cantilever wing fitted with flaps and leading edge slats. That the resultant aircraft now looks so ordinary is testimony to the far-sightedness of Messerschmitt and his team, for the single-seat low winged monoplane they produced established a convention in fighter design that set the standards for much of the decade that followed.

INITIAL FLIGHT

The prototype of the new fighter, the Bayerische Flugzeugwerke Bf 109, made its maiden flight from Augsburg-Haunstetten in September 1935 with "Bubi" Knoetsch at the controls. Although the aircraft had been designed around the 610hp Jumo 210 twelve-cylinder inverted-Vee liquid cooled engine, one was not available at that time and, ironically in view of later events, the prototype took off powered by a 695hp Rolls-Royce Kestrel imported from Britain.

On completion of its initial flight trials at Augsburg, the prototype was flown to the Luftwaffe test centre at Rechlin. There the fighter's service career got off to an inauspicious start, for as the Bf 109 touched-down the attachment point for the starboard undercarriage leg fractured, causing it to make a spectacular arrival. Fortunately for the company, the airframe suffered only superficial damage and this was soon repaired.

Competing with the Bf 109 for the Luftwaffe contract were three other monoplane fighters: the Arado Ar 80, the Heinkel He 112 and the Focke Wulf Fw 159. Messerschmitt's design quickly demonstrated that it had a clear edge over the others in terms of performance: its maximum level speed of 290mph (467kmh) was 17mph faster than the next contender, the He 112, and it was also faster in the dive and in the climb. The Ar 80, with a fixed undercarriage, and the Fw 159, with a strut-braced high wing, were pedestrian designs of relatively low performance and both were quickly eliminated from the competition.

Following the initial service trials at Rechlin, the Luftwaffe placed orders for 10 prototypes each of the Bf 109 and the He 112. Despite the superior performance of the former, the Heinkel design was preferred for its lower wing loading, the better view from the cockpit for both take-off and

Left: The first prototype of the Bf 109, the V1, undergoing ground engine runs at the time of its maiden flight in 1935.

landing, and its greater stability on the ground conferred by the wide-track undercarriage.

In January 1936 a second prototype Bf 109A, the V2 powered by the Jumo 210A engine, joined the test programme. This aircraft was much the same as the first prototype, except that the airframe was strengthened in some areas, particularly around the undercarriage. The V3 flew in June 1936 and was the first Bf 109 to carry armament; it was fitted with two MG17 7.9mm machine guns mounted along the top of the engine and synchronized to fire through the propeller.

The definitive evaluation undertaken by the Luftwaffe to select the new monoplane fighter took place at Travemünde in the Autumn of 1936; and following a series of impressive demonstration flights by Hermann Wurster the Messerschmitt design was selected for large scale production.

Meanwhile, the Luftwaffe had asked for increased firepower from the new fighter. As a result, the V4, which flew in November 1936, was fitted with a third machine gun mounted between the cylinder banks of the Jumo 210 engine and firing through the airscrew spinner. The V4 became the prototype of the Bf 109B, the initial version of the fighter selected for production. The third weapon was omitted from production aircraft when firing trials with the engine-mounted gun revealed that it was liable to overheat and seize up after firing a few rounds.

Right, from top to bottom: the first prototype, V1, powered by a Rolls-Royce Kestrel engine; the prototype of the Bf 109B, the V4, which was the first production version; the V8 which was fitted with the Jumo 210 fuel-injection engine; and the V13 with a sprint version of the DB 601 engine which raised the world speed record to 379mph (611kmh).

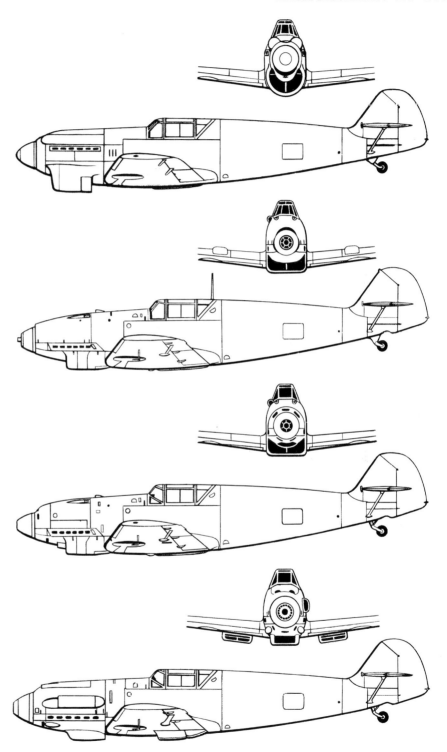

History and Development

Above: A Bf 109B showing off its distinctive angular wing form. When the type entered service in 1937, it was without doubt the most potent fighter aircraft there was in the world.

Tooling up for the Bf 109B-1 assembly line at Augsburg began in the autumn of 1936, but even before the first production aircraft emerged from the factory events abroad led to the diversion of some aircraft from the test programme. In the summer of 1936 the Luftwaffe had despatched a multi-role combat force, the Condor Legion, to assist the Nationalist forces fighting in the Spanish Civil War. In a counter-move the Soviet Union began supplying modern aircraft to the Republican Air Force, and that Autumn German fighter pilots were disconcerted to discover that the Polikarpov I-15s and I-16s flown by the enemy had a clear edge over their Heinkel He 51 biplanes.

To determine whether the Bf 109 could retrieve the situation, the German Air Ministry made the brave decision to ship three prototypes (the V3, V4 and V5) to Spain for trials under combat conditions. The aircraft were re-assembled at Seville-Tablada and flew from there. Inevitably, there were severe problems in trying to operate non-production aircraft under such primitive conditions; serviceability was poor for a start and this greatly restricted flying. It is believed that none of the prototypes had had any

encounter with enemy aircraft before the trial ended in February 1937 and all three were shipped back to Germany. Although the trial highlighted the difficulties of trying to operate modern fighter types from landing grounds in Spain, it showed that with proper support it was possible. Front-line pilots who flew the monoplane fighter had no doubt that it was far superior to the opposing fighters, and they made strong representations for production Bf 109s to be sent to Spain as soon as they became available.

In February 1937 the first production Bf 109B-1 emerged from the factory at Augsburg. The first Luftwaffe unit to receive the new fighter was II Gruppe of Jagdgeschwader 132 based at Jueterbog-Damm. Simultaneously, however, 16 of the new "Bertha"

Below: A line-up of early production Bf 109Bs at the Bayerische Flugzeugwerke plant at Augsburg in early 1937 await their delivery to various units of the fledgling Luftwaffe.

fighters were crated and shipped to war-torn Spain to equip 2 Staffel of Jagdgruppe 88 commanded by Oberleutnant Guenther Luetzow.

Although 2/J88 was declared operational in April 1937, it was not until July that the Bf 109 received its baptism of fire when Republican forces went onto the offensive west of Madrid. During the air actions that followed, the primary mission of the Bf 109s was to escort Junkers Ju 52 bombers which were attacking targets in the battle area.

In the resultant air combats, the Bf 109 proved faster than the I-16 (the best fighter operated by the Republicans) at all altitudes; it had a higher operational ceiling, it was faster in the dive and was generally superior above 10,000ft (3,048m). For its part, the I-16 could out-turn and out-climb the Bf 109B and was marginally the better fighter below 10,000ft. In combat the Republican pilots would try to lure their opponents into dogfights below 10,000ft, but with little success. The Bf 109 pilots quickly learned that

Above: A Luftwaffe pilot of the Condor Legion in Spain employs a local but older and far less rapid form of transport.

Right: A Bf 109B of 2 Staffel of Jagdgruppe 88 (2/J88) during the Spanish Civil War. The Bf 109 outclassed Soviet I-15s and I-16s.

their superior performance at high-altitude usually gave them the luxury of accepting combat on their terms, or declining it until they had moved in-to a position of advantage. They would swoop on their opponents from above, deliver their attack, then zoom back to altitude before setting up the next attack. Provided they maintained speed and stuck to these tactics the Bf 109s were almost invincible. In a war in which relatively few aircraft took part, the force of well-handled modern fighters had an effect out of all pro-portion to its numbers.

In September 1937 Guenther Luetzow moved to command 1/J88 in order to oversee the conversion of that unit from He 51s to Bf 109s. Oberleutnant Joachim Schlichting replaced him as commander of 2/J88. Schlichting, who was credited with five aerial victories over Spain, told this author that although the Bf 109B-1 outwardly resembled the later, more formidable versions of the fighter, in some respects it was still a primitive aircraft. Initially, the fighter was fitted with a fixed-pitch propeller which made for poor ac-celeration during take-off from the

SPECIFICATION

Bf109 B-1

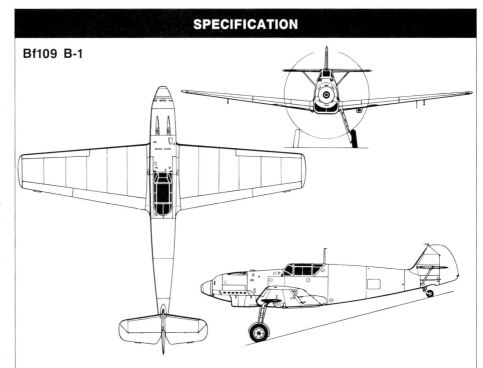

Dimensions
Length: 29ft 0½in (8.85m)
Wing span: 32ft 4½in (9.87m)
Gross wing area: 174sq ft (16.17m²)

Weights
Empty: 3,319lb (1,505kg)
Normal take-off: 4,741lb (2,150kg)

Power
1 x Junkers Jumo 210 Da liquid-cooled
12-cylinder inverted-Vee piston engine

rated at 635hp

Performance
Maximum speed: 255mph (410km/h) at sea level, 289mph (465km/h) at 13,100ft (4,000m)
Maximum rate of climb: 19,700ft (6,000m) in 9min 48 sec

Service ceiling: 26,900ft (8,200m)
Maximum range (without reserves): 428 miles (690km)

History and Development

uneven Spanish airfields. The guns were cocked using levers in the cockpit, and fired by a lever pulling a cable connected to the triggers, as had been the case with First World War aircraft. The radio equipment fitted to the early Bf 109s was unreliable, it gave poor reception and often it was left off by the pilots.

Some of the fiercest aerial fighting of the war in Spain took place during the Republican offensive in the Teruel area early in 1938. On 7 Feburary Hauptmann Gotthardt Handrick, now the commander of Jagdgruppe 88, was leading the Bf 109s from both Staffeln on a bomber escort mission. Near Teruel he sighted a formation of 22 Soviet built Tupolev SB-2 bombers, and a careful search of the sky revealed no sign of Republican fighters in the area. Handrick led his fighters in an attack on the enemy aircraft and several bombers were shot down before a score of I-16 fighters arrived on the scene and a swirling dogfight followed. When the action ended the Bf 109s had destroyed ten enemy bombers and two fighters for no loss to themselves.

Left, from top to bottom: A Bf 109D-1 wearing the markings of the gruppenkommandeur of II/ZG 26 Horst Wessel, based at Werl in August 1939.

An ex-Condor Legion Bf 109B employed as a fighter trainer by the Spanish Escuela de Caza.

A Bf 109B transferred to the Spanish Nationalist air arm at Logrono in April 1939.

A Bf 109B-2 flown by 2/J88's Hpt. Handrick prior to its transfer to the Ejercito del Aire.

A Bf 109B-2 sporting the standard early markings of the famous Jagdgruppe 88.

(Elsewhere that day, Leutnant Wilhelm Balthasar engaged a force of Republican bombers and their escorts and shot down three bombers and one fighter within a space of just six minutes.)

NEW FIGHTER TACTICS

Much has been written about the effectiveness of the air fighting tactics, based on fighters flying in loose pairs or fours, developed by Bf 109 pilots flying in Spain. According to Joachim Schlichting, who commanded 2/J88 for a time, the new tactics came about almost by accident. The He 51 fighters had used the "Kette" (three-aircaft formation) and 2/J88 would have too but for the shortage of serviceable Bf 109s which meant that rarely were more than six fighters available for a mission. During escort missions the fighters were divided into three sub-units; one of which flew ahead of the bombers, one flew behind and one flew about 3,000ft (900m) above the bombers. Initially, that requirement dictated the use of the two-aircraft fighting unit for Bf 109s. The wingman flew about 40yds (36m) to one side of his leader, somewhat further than in the "Kette" but still close enough to observe his leader's hand signals. Thus was borne the "Rotte" or fighting pair. Pilots soon discovered that a two-aircraft fighting unit was easier to handle during high-speed combat than one with three.

When more Bf 109s became available, two "Rotten" combined to form a four-aircraft "Pulk" (the term "Schwarm" did not come into use until later). When Oberleutnant Werner Moelders arrived in Spain in the Summer of 1938, he and other pilots improved on these tactics but by then the value of the "Rotte" and "Pulk" fighting formations had been firmly established and were to be employed to devastating effect.

Top: A Schwarm formation of Bf 109Es from I/JG2 Richthofen over the English Channel wearing markings typical of those from the Battle of Britain period.

WORLD RECORD

Meanwhile, in November 1937 the Bf 109 had achieved world-wide acclaim when it captured the world landplane speed record. The V13 was specially modified for the attempt and fitted with a sprint version of the DB601 engine, developing a maximum of 1,650hp for short periods. Hermann Wurster flew the aircraft over the course approved by the Fedération Aéronautique Internationale (FAI). He

Above: A Swiss Bf 109E-3 of Fliegerkompagnie 6 based at Thun in 1939. This aircraft crashed into a mountain at Schallenburg in 1942, killing the pilot.

flew the 1.86 miles (3km) twice in each direction, at altitudes below 246ft (75m), achieving an average speed over the four runs of 379mph (611kmh). (The world's absolute speed record was held by the Italian Macchi-Castoldi MC 72 floatplane which had flown at 440mph (709kmh), far beyond the reach of the modified fighter.)

Impressive performances led to export orders and the Swiss took a number of the Jumo-engined Cs and returned in 1940 for 80 E-1 and E-3s.

The next major production version was the Bf 109C-1, similar to the B version but powered by the Jumo 210Ga engine with fuel injection. Firepower was increased to four guns, with the addition of two in the wing close to the root and synchronized to fire through the airscrew. The first C-1s began leaving the production lines early in 1938 and, as with the previous version, aircraft of the first batches were sent to J88 in Spain. The C-2 which followed featured the four-gun armament of the C-1 and reinstated the weapon firing through the propeller spinner. To cool the weapon, air was drawn in from a scoop mounted on top of the engine cowling.

The Bf 109D was powered by the 960hp Daimler Benz DB 600 engine, giving a maximum speed of 356mph (574kmh) at 11,400ft (3,500m). The D-1 carried an armament of two MG 17 machine guns and one MG FF 20mm cannon firing through the propeller spinner. When its DB 600

Top: A Bf 109C-2 of 10 (N)/JG26 based at Jever in the autumn of 1939. At this time, as the (N) suggests, the unit operated in the night interception role, but later reverted to daylight work.

Above: A Bf 109C-2 of JG102 based at Bernburg. The unit was later re-designated I/ZG2 and re-equipped with Bf 110s. Note the Bernburger Hunter emblem visible above the wing.

worked properly the D version gave an impressive performance, but the engine suffered from numerous teething troubles and its reliability was poor. Less than 200 examples of this version of the fighter were built before it was passed out of production.

A small number of ''Doras'', as they were known, were sent to J88 in Spain and in August 1938 this version went into action. Overall, the number of Bf 109s sent to Spain was never large. Up to the beginning of

Left: A line-up of brand new Bf 109C-2s outside the Focke-Wulf factory at Bremen. This version was armed with five MG 17s, one firing through the propeller.

Bf 109 Fighter Gruppen
Units fully or partially equippd with the Bf 109 at the time of the Munich Crisis in September 1938:

Jagdgruppe 88	Spain
I/JG 131	Jesau
I/JG 132	Doeberitz
II/JG 132	Jueterbog-Damm
I/JG 136	Eger-Marienbad
I/JG 234	Cologne
II/JG 234	Dusseldorf
I/JG 334	Wiesbaden

Warnemuende and those of Erla at Leipzig, Fieseler at Kassel and Focke Wulf at Bremen.

In September 1938 the Munich Crisis broke out with Hitler laying claim to the Sudetenland area of Czechoslovakia. That month the Luftwaffe Quartermaster General's records listed a total of 583 Bf 109s of all versions on strength, of which just 510 were serviceable. Later versions of the fighter were then becoming available in large numbers, but the ''Bertha'' was still the most numerous of those in service. Eight Gruppen had equipped, or were in the process of re-equipping, with the Bf 109. Many writers have repeated the line that the British government had to capitulate to Hitler's demand for territory in order to buy time for the country to re-arm, yet it can be seen that in

December 1938 only 55 Bs, Cs and Ds had been delivered to the Condor Legion, of which 37 were then serving with Jagdgruppe 88. Nevertheless, by that time the Nationalist Air Force and its allies had secured complete air superiority.

By the summer of 1938 the success of the Bf 109 fighter was assured and the management of the Bayerische Flugzeugwerke decided to capitalize on the name of the now-famous chief designer. Willy Messerschmitt was appointed Chairman and Managing Director of the company, and its name was changed to Messerschmitt AG. The new name would be applied to subsequent aircraft designs built by the company, but the Bf 109 and other aircraft built previously would retain the 'Bf' designation in official sources.

During 1938 the Luftwaffe was expanding rapidly and there was a massive increase in the number of Bf 109s built. As well as two Messerschmitt-owned factories, Bf 109s were disgorging from the Arado plant at

Top, right: After the civil war, JG88 passed its Bf 109Bs to the newly formed Spanish Ejercito del Aire. This one is being used as a trainer in 1947.

Right: A Bf 109D belonging to JG152. This version was armed with a 0.8in (20mm) Oerlikon FF cannon which fired through the propeller hub.

Combat

September 1938 the Luftwaffe fighter force was not in any condition to fight a major war (its bomber arm was in no better state). At the time, the German propaganda line about their nation's omnipotent air strength was widely believed, and it was so successful that even more than fifty years later it continues to be repeated.

By the close of 1938 the Republican forces in Spain were fast approaching collapse. Fighters of the Condor Legion had their final encounter with enemy aircraft on 31 January 1939 and the force flew its last operational mission on 27 March 1939, with the remaining enemy forces surrendering on the following day. After the cease-fire the Condor Legion passed all 47 of its Bf 109s to the new Spanish Air Force. Twenty of the fighters were brand new Bf 109Es ("Emils") that had arrived just too late to see combat. The rest were the B, C and D models that had survived combat.

THE "EMIL"

As stated, the D version of the Bf 109 would have been a formidable fighter but for the unreliability of its engine. The next developmental type was far

better; known as the E or "Emil" it was the first to be built in really large numbers. The V-14 aircraft, prototype for this version, was powered by the new Daimler Benz DB 601 engine. This aircraft carried an armament of two MG 17 7.9mm machine guns in the fuselage and two MG FF 20mm cannon in the wings, though early production "Emils" would revert to the four MG 17 machine gun armament fitted to earlier variants. The first Bf 109E-1s were delivered to the

Above, left: This picture offers a good view of the revised nose contours and enlarged spinner of the Bf 109F which first appeared on the Bf 109V-23.

Above: A good close-up of the compact engine mounting of the Daimler Benz DB 601. Note the downard pointing cylinder banks on this inverted-Vee motor.

Left: A scramble take-off of a Bf 109E-1 in the summer of 1939. The aircraft bears the Scalded Cat emblem of 2/JG20 which was later re-designated 8/JG51.

Luftwaffe early in 1939 and with production of the Bf 109 running at about 130 per month the "Emil" rapidly replaced the earlier versions of the fighter then serving with many of the front line units.

The Luftwaffe Quartermaster General's list for 2 September 1939, the day following the invasion of Poland, reveals that the force had 1,081 Bf 109s on strength, of which 979 were serviceable. At that time some 24 fighter Gruppen and five Staffeln were

Right, from top to bottom: A Bf 109D serving as an operational trainer with Jagdfliegerschule 1 based at Werneuchen in 1940. Note the ejector-type exhaust.

A Bf 109E-1 of I/JG1 based at Seerappen in August 1939. The E model took the Bf 109 to the fore of fighter development, proving faster than the Spitfire although it was less agile.

A Bf 109E-1 of IV/JG132 Richthofen (later I/JG77) based at Werneuchen in early 1939. Note the Wanderzirkus Jahnke emblem of the unit painted onto the nose of the aircraft.

A Bf 109E-1 of II/JG26 Schlageter based at Dusseldorf in August 1939 and wearing white soluble tail paint for easy removal after flying on exercises.

Above: Early Bf 109Es were armed for firepower with four 0.5in (7.9mm) MG 17 guns. The later Bf 110 had all four in the nose, as seen here, but the ''Emil'' had only two with two in the wings.

equipped with the Bf 109. The most numerous version in service was the ''Emil'', which equipped 15 Gruppen and one Staffel and partially equipped two more Gruppen. At this time seven Zerstoerergruppen operated Bf 109Bs, Cs and Ds on a temporary basis until their intended Bf 110 twin-engined fighters became available; the remaining units operated Bf 109Cs.

THE POLISH CAMPAIGN

Contrary to popular legend, only a small proportion of the Bf 109 force took part in the Polish campaign — five Gruppen, with less than 200 serviceable aircraft, out of 24 Gruppen then equipped with the type. The bulk of the force was held back in western Germany to meet a possible onslaught

Combat

Bf 109 FRONT LINE UNITS, 2 SEPTEMBER 1939			

Units marked with asterisk took part in the Polish campaign.
First figure refers to aircraft total, second figure indicates the numbers serviceable.

Lehrdivision
Lehr Geschwader 2

Stab	3	3	Bf 109E*
I Gruppe	36	34	Bf 109E*
10 Staffel	12	9	Bf 109E

Luftflotte 1 (north-eastern Germany)
Jagdgeschwader 1

I Gruppe	54	54	Bf 109E*

Jagdgeschwader 2

II Gruppe	42	39	Bf 109E*
10 Staffel	9	9	Bf 109C, night fighting unit

Jagdgeschwader 3

Stab	3	3	Bf 109E
I Gruppe	48	42	Bf 109E

Jagdgeschwader 20

I Gruppe	21	20	Bf 109E

Jagdgeschwader 21

I Gruppe	29	28	Bf 109C and E*

Zerstoerergeschwader 1

II Gruppe	36	36	Bf 109B* (a)

Zerstoerergeschwader 2

I Gruppe	44	40	Bf 109D* (a)

Luftflotte 2 (north-western Germany)
Jagdgeschwader 26

I Gruppe	48	48	Bf 109E
II Gruppe	48	44	Bf 109E
10 Staffel	10	8	Bf 109C, night fighting unit

Zerstoerergeschwader 26

I Gruppe	52	46	Bf 109B and D (a)
II Gruppe	48	47	Bf 109B and D (a)
III Gruppe	48	44	Bf 109B and C (a)

Luftflotte 3 (south-western Germany)
Jagdgeschwader 51

I Gruppe	47	39	Bf 109E

Jagdgeschwader 52

I Gruppe	39	34	Bf 109E

Jagdgeschwader 53

I Gruppe	51	39	Bf 109E
II Gruppe	43	41	Bf 109E

Jagdgeschwader 70

I Gruppe	24	24	Bf 109E

Jagdgeschwader 71

I Gruppe	39	18	Bf 109C and E

Zerstoerergeschwader 52

I Gruppe	44	43	Bf 109B (a)

Luftflotte 4 (south-eastern Germany)
Jagdgeschwader 76

I Gruppe	49	45	Bf 109E

Jagdgeschwader 77

I Gruppe	50	43	Bf 109E
II Gruppe	50	36	Bf 109E

Zerstoerergeschwader 76

II Gruppe	40	39	Bf 109B and C

Assigned to Navy
Traegergruppe 186

5, 6 Staffeln	24	24	Bf 109C (b)

(a) Unit formed to operate with Bf 110 twin-engined fighter, but operated Bf 109s until these became available.
(b) Unit operating standard Bf 109Cs, formed to train pilots earmarked to operate the fully navalized Bf 109T version from the aircraft carrier *Graf Zeppelin*.

Left: A Bf 109E of III/JG27; note the oversized wing markings on the upper surfaces, painted to aid recognition after several friendly-fire incidents.

Above: A Bf 109E-1 on a combat patrol wearing a speckled camouflage paint finish which is typical of the 1940 period when this picture was taken.

by the Royal Air Force (RAF) and the French Air Force — a threat that never materialized.

The 200-odd Bf 109s that did support the attack on Poland proved to be sufficient to counter the weak Polish Air Force. The latter possessed only about 150 fighters and a similar number of bombers, most of them obsolescent types. The best Polish fighter, the PZL 11, had a maximum speed of only 242mph (389kmh) at 16,200ft (4,900m) and was no match even for the early versions of the Bf 109. Completely outclassed by the ''Emil'', these fighters fell as easy prey whenever the two met in combat.

Within a couple of weeks the Polish Air Force was virtually out of the fight, and before the land campaign ended on 28 September the Luftwaffe felt sufficiently secure to pull two Bf 109 Gruppen out and re-position them for the defence of Germany.

OFFENSIVE IN THE WEST

Meanwhile, in the west, there was small-scale aerial activity as each side probed the strengths and weaknesses of the other. On 30 September the RAF learned a hard lesson when a formation of five Fairey Battle single-engined bombers was attacked while carrying out a daylight armed reconnaissance over the Saarbrucken area. Bf 109E-1s of JG 53 which rose to engage them quickly shot down four out of the five for no loss to themselves. For the remainder of the ''The Phoney War'' the Battles would confine their operations over German territory to the hours of darkness. But the incident was a grim portent of the fate awaiting them in the following spring, when sheer military necessity would next force them to mount daylight operations against heavily defended targets.

In another significant action near the end of the year, the Bf 109 demonstrated its superiority against the best-armed bomber type in the RAF. On 18 December 1939, a force of 24 Wellingtons flew down the coast off Wilhelmshaven with orders to attack any German warships found at sea. The bombers flew in close formation, relying on the combined crossfire from their gun turrets to protect them if enemy fighters attacked. Thirty-four Bf 109Bs, Cs and Es from 10/JG 26, II/JG 77 and II/ZG 1, together with 16 Bf 110s, took off to engage and in the swirling fight that followed 12 Wellingtons were shot down and two more were damaged so seriously that they crashed on landing. Only two Bf 109s were shot down during the engagement. Thus it was that the RAF learned the hard way, as other air forces would learn later, that unescorted bomber formations could not survive in the face of determined attack by modern fighters. Following this action, the RAF made the policy decision that

Above: Armourers feed ammunition into the magazine of an MG 17 mounted in the wing of a BF 109E-1. Cleanliness was vital, for any dirt or grit on the rounds might cause a stoppage.

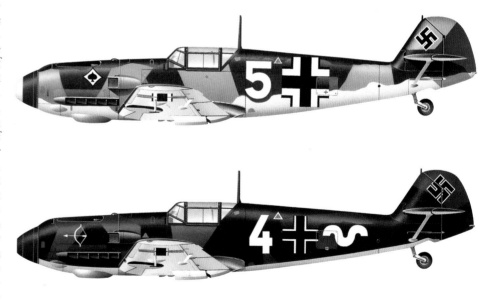

Top: A Bf 109E-1 of I/JG53 Pik As, based at Wiesbaden-Erbenheim during the winter of 1939-40. Note the Ace of Spades emblem.

Above: A Bf 109E-1 of III/JG 51 based at Bonninghardt in April 1940. The bow and arrow emblem is that of 7/JG51.

Combat

Messerschmitt Bf 109 E-4 cutaway drawing key

1 Hollow propeller Hub
2 Spinner
3 Three-blade VDM variable pitch propeller
4 Propeller pitch-change mechanism
5 Spinner back plate
6 Glycol coolant header tank
7 Glycol filler cap
8 Cowling fastener
9 Chin intake
10 Coolant pipe fairing
11 Exhaust forward fairing
12 Additional (long-range) oil tank
13 Daimler-Benz DB 601A engine
14 Supplementary intakes
15 Fuselage machine gun troughs
16 Anti-vibration engine mounting pads
17 Exhaust ejector stubs
18 Coolant pipes (to underwing radiators)
19 Oil cooler intake
20 Coolant radiator
21 Radiator outlet flap
22 Cowling frame
23 Engine mounting support strut
24 Spent cartridge collector compartment
25 Ammunition boxes (starboard loading)
26 Engine supercharger
27 Supercharger air intake fairing
28 Forged magnesium alloy cantilever engine mounting
29 Engine mounting/forward bulkhead attachment
30 Ammunition feed chutes
31 Engine accessories
32 Two fuselage-mounted MG17 machine guns
33 Blast tube muzzles
34 Wing skinning
35 Starboard cannon access
36 20mm MG FF wing cannon
37 Leading-edge automatic slot
38 Slot tracks
39 Slot acuating linkage
40 Wing main spar
41 Intermediate rib station
42 Wing end rib
43 Starboard navigation light
44 Aileron outer hinge
45 Aileron metal trim tab
46 Starboard aileron
47 Aileron/flap link connection
48 Combined control linkage
49 Starboard flap frame
50 Cannon ammunition drum access
51 Fuselage machine gun cooling slots
52 Gun mounting frame
53 Firewall/bulkhead
54 Instrument panel near face (fabric covered)
55 Oil dipstick cover
56 Control column
57 Oil filler cap (tank omitted for clarity)
58 Rudder pedal assembly
59 Aircraft identity data plate (external)
60 main spar centre-section carry-through
61 Underfloor control linkage
62 Oxygen regulator

63 Harness adjustment lever
64 Engine priming pump
65 Circuit breaker panel
66 Hood catch
67 Starboard hinged cockpit canopy
68 Revi gunsight (offset to starboard)
69 Windscreen panel frame
70 Canopy section frame
71 Pilot's head armour
72 Pilot's back armour
73 Seat harness
74 Pilot's seat
75 Seat adjustment lever
76 Tailplane incidence handwheel
77 Cockpit floor diaphragm
78 Landing flaps control handwheel
79 Seat support frame
80 Contoured (''L'' shape) fuel tank
81 Tailplane incidence cables
82 Fuselage frame
83 Rudder cable
84 Oxygen cylinders (2)
85 Fuel filler/overspill pipes
86 Baggage compartment
87 Entry handhold (spring loaded)
88 Canopy fixed aft section
89 Aerial mast
90 Aerial
91 Fuel filler cap
92 Fuel vent line
93 Radio pack support brackets
94 Anti-vibration bungee supports
95 FuG VII transmitter/receiver radio pack
96 Aerial lead-in
97 Tailplane incidence cable pulley
98 Rudder control cable
99 Monocoque fuselage structure
100 Radio access/first aid kit panel
101 Elevator control cables

102 Fuselage frame
103 Lifting tube
104 Tailfin root fillet
105 Tailplane incidence gauge (external)
106 Tailplane support strut
107 Starboard tailplane
108 Elevator outer-hinge
109 Elevator balance
110 Starboard elevator
111 Tailfin structure
112 Aerial stub
113 Rudder balance
114 Rudder upper hinge
115 Rudder frame
116 Rudder trim tab
117 Tail navigation light
118 Port elevator frame
119 Elevator balance
120 Rudder control quadrant
121 Tailplane structure
122 Elevator torque tube sleeve
123 Tailplane end rib attachment
124 Fuselage end post
125 Elevator control pod

126 Port tailplane support strut
127 Non-retractable tailwheel
128 Tailwheel leg
129 Elevator control cable/rod link
130 Tailwheel shock-absorber
131 Rudder control cable
132 Fuselage stringer
133 Accumulator
134 Fuselage half ventral join
135 Electrical leads
136 Fuselage panels
137 Radio pack lower support frames
138 Entry foothold (spring loaded)
139 Wingroot fillet
140 Flap profile
141 Port flap frame
142 Port aileron frame
143 Aileron metal trim tab
144 Rear spar
145 Port wingtip
146 Port navigation light
147 Wing main spar outer section

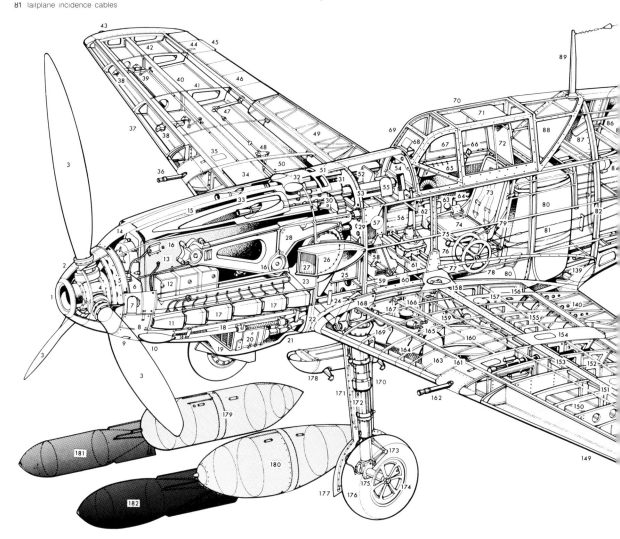

148 Solid ribs
149 Leading-edge automatic slot
150 Rib cut-outs
151 Control link access plate
152 Wing rib stations
153 Port wing 20mm MG FF cannon installation
154 Ammunition drum access panel
155 Inboard rib cut-outs
156 Flap visual position indicator
157 Control access panel
158 Main spar/fuselage attachment fairing
159 Wing control surface cable pulleys
160 Port mainwheel well
161 Wheel well (zipped) fabric shield
162 20mm MG FF wing cannon
163 Wing front spar
164 Undercarriage leg tunnel rib cut-outs
165 Undercarriage lock mechanism
166 Wing/fuselage end rib
167 Undercarriage actuating cylinder
168 Mainwheel leg/fuselage attachment bracket
169 Leg pivot point
170 Mainwheel oleo leg
171 Mainwheel leg door
172 Brake lines
173 Torque links
174 Mainwheel hub
175 Axle
176 Port mainwheel
177 Mainwheel half-door
178 Ventral ETC centre-line stores pylon possible loads inc.
179 Early-type (wooden) drop tank
180 66 Imp gal (300l) (Junkers) metal drop tank
181 551lb (250kg) HE bomb or
182 551lb (250kg) SAP bomb

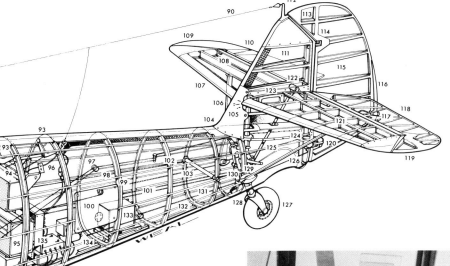

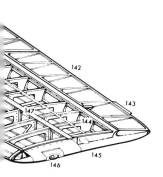

in future most of its attacks on Germany would be made by night.

The new Bf 109E was not prominent during the occupation of Denmark and Norway but on 10 May 1940 German forces launched the offensive in the west for which they had prepared long and hard. By then the Luftwaffe's 1,346 Bf 109s were serving with front line units, of which just over one thousand were serviceable. One-quarter of these aircraft were held back to defend targets in Germany, the other three-quarters were assigned to Luftflotten 2 and 3 supporting the offensive campaign.

During the campaign in the west, the Luftwaffe quickly established air superiority over the Dutch, Belgian and French Air Forces, as well as the RAF squadrons based in France. Almost unhindered by Allied fighters, the German bombers and dive-bombers cleared a path for fast-moving Panzer divisions to storm across France and sever the Allied armies in the north of the country from those in the south. Relatively few Bf 109s were lost in combat and only at the end of the campaign, during the Dunkirk evacuation, was there much in the way of fighter-versus-fighter combat. Oberleutnant Julius Neumann, who flew with Jagdgeschwader 27, remembers: "During the campaign in France it was difficult to compare our (Bf) 109 with the French Morane or Curtiss fighters, because I never had a dogfight with either of them. I saw only one Morane during the entire campaign and it was disappearing in the distance. Our Geschwader had very little dogfighting experience until the Dunkirk action, where we met the RAF for the first

Left: The instrument panel and cramped cockpit of a Bf 109E. Despite the untidy layout of the instruments, the pilots came to love this capable fighter.

Combat

time in numbers. Our pilots came back with the highest respect for the (new) enemy.''

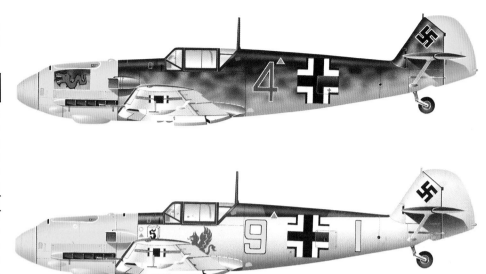

BATTLE OF BRITAIN

The action during the period which became known as The Battle of Britain opened in July 1940 with attacks on shipping passing through the English Channel. Typical of the scrappy actions of the time was that on the afternoon of 13 July when a convoy of freighters passed through the Straits of Dover. Half a dozen Ju 87s from Sturzkampfgeschwader 1 were in the process of dive-bombing the ships when they came under attack from eleven Hurricanes of No 56 Squadron.

SPECIFICATION

Bf109 E-3

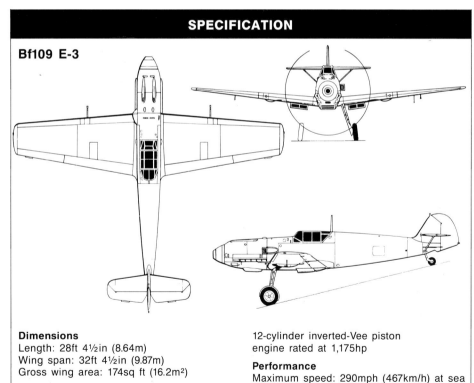

Dimensions
Length: 28ft 4½in (8.64m)
Wing span: 32ft 4½in (9.87m)
Gross wing area: 174sq ft (16.2m²)

Weights
Empty: 4,189lb (1,900kg)
Normal take-off: 5,875lb (2,665kg)

Power
1 x Daimler Benz DB601A liquid-cooled

12-cylinder inverted-Vee piston engine rated at 1,175hp

Performance
Maximum speed: 290mph (467km/h) at sea level,
348mph (560km/h) at 14,560ft (4,440m)
Initial rate of climb: 3,280ft/min (16.66m/sec)
Service ceiling: 34,450ft (10,500ft)
Maximum range: 410 miles (660km)

Top: A Bf 109E-3 of I/JG3 Udet based at Colombert, France, during the Battle of Britain. The dragon is 2/JG3's emblem.

Above: A Bf 109E-3 of III/JG26 Schlageter based at Caffiers, France. The fierce-looking dragon emblem is that of 9/JG26.

Major Josef Foezoe was leading the Staffel of Bf 109s of II/JG 51 escorting the Stukas: ''Unfortunately for them (the Hurricanes), they slid into position directly between the Stukas and our close-escort Messerschmitts. We opened fire, and at once three Hurricanes separated from the formation, two dropping and one gliding down to the water smoking heavily. At that instant I saw a Stuka diving in an attempt to reach the French coast. It was chased by a single Hurricane. Behind the Hurricane was a 109, and behind that a second Hurricane, all of the fighters firing at the aircraft in front. I saw the deadly dangerous situation and rushed down. There were five aircraft diving in line towards the water. The Stuka was badly hit and both crewmen wounded; it crashed on the beach near Wissant. The leading Messerschmitt, flown by Feldwebel John, shot down the first Hurricane into the water, its right wing appeared above the waves like the dorsal fin of a shark before it sank. My Hurricane dropped like a stone close to the one that John had shot down.'' No 56 Squadron lost two Hurricanes destroyed and two damaged. On the German side two Ju 87s were seriously damaged but JG 51 suffered no losses.

Six days later, on 19 July, the Bf 109 established its superiority over the RAF's Defiant turret fighter. As nine of these fighters belonging to No 141 Squadron were moving in to protect a convoy under attack, they were ''bounced'' from out of the sun by Bf 109s, again from JG 51. A one-sided action followed and only the timely arrival of a squadron of Hurricanes saved the Defiants from complete annihilation. Only three turret fighters survived the encounter, one with serious damage, while one Bf 109 was shot down. Following this action the Defiant played only a minor part in the daylight air battles over the south of England.

During the initial phase of the Battle of Britain the Bf 109 units flew several ''Freijagd'' or free hunting sweeps over southern England, aiming to draw RAF fighters into action. Initially, these operations had some success, but when the nature of the German tactics became clear the defending fighter-controllers received orders to engage only against those formations thought to contain bombers. Whenever possible, the fighter sweeps were left well alone.

AGAINST THE BEST

On 13 August the German attack shifted to airfields in southern England but the early actions brought home to the Luftwaffe the clear lesson that unescorted bombers operating by day

Top: A group of Bf 109Es from II/JG27 patrolling during the early stages of the Battle of Britain when the unit was based at Crepon in western France as part of Luftflotte 3.

Above: A pair of Bf 109Es still in factory markings, probably photographed during a delivery flight from the manufacturers to a forward-based aircraft park prior to their use in combat.

Combat

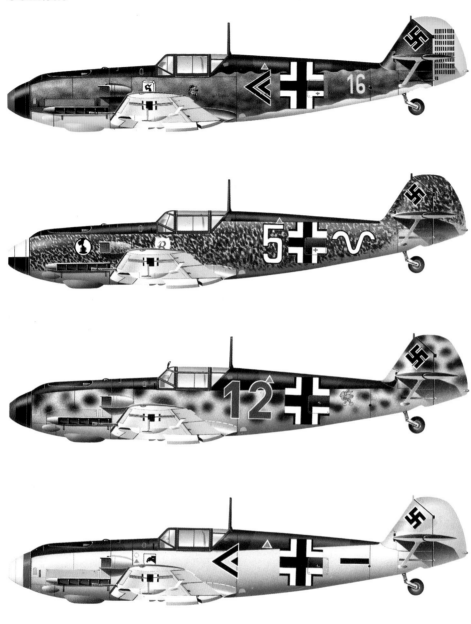

Left, from top to bottom: A Bf 109E-3 flown by Obt. Adolf Galland of JG26. Note his personal Mickey Mouse motif and the 83 kill bars on the rudder.

A Bf 109E-3 of III/JG2 Richthofen based in France during May-June 1940. Note the three Richthofen insignia.

A Bf 109E-3 of I/LG2 based at Calais-Marck in August 1940 sports the Mickey Mouse emblem of 3 Staffel.

A Bf 109E-3 of Hpt. Henschel, Gruppenkommandeur of II/JG77 based at Aalborg, Norway, in July of 1940.

cutting out. British fighters were fitted with float carburettors, and if their pilots attempted to imitate these manoeuvres the engine would cut out due to fuel starvation. Thus a common method used by Bf 109s to rid themselves of pursuing British fighters was to push hard on the stick to bunt the aircraft, and then dive away. Such marginal differences could decide a few combats, but they should not cloud the overall picture.

Range too was also a factor. The E had shortcomings in this area and the long-range Bf 110 was supposed to fly protective escort for the bombers; in reality the Bf 110 was a failure. The Bf 109, however, soon came into service with the suitably equipped E-7 version in August 1940 and this proved a success, although many actually had to protect the Bf 110s!

One cliché image of the Battle of Britain is a sky full of Bf 109s and Spitfires and/or Hurricanes engaged in turning combats with individual enemy fighters. That makes for a spectacular painting with lots of room for artists' licence, but it is far from the truth. Any pilot who concentrated his

over southern England could expect short shrift if they were caught by British fighters. During the action, the strengths and weaknesses of the Bf 109E, when compared with the RAF's Spitfire and Hurricane fighters, quickly became evident. Both British fighters could out-turn the Bf 109, and below about 15,000ft (about 4,600m)

the Spitfire was the faster. Above 20,000ft (6,100m) the Bf 109E was faster than the Spitfire, and it could outrun the Hurricane at any altitude. A futher advantage enjoyed by Bf 109 pilots was that the fuel injection system of the DB 601 engine allowed them to fly manoeuvres involving negative gravity (G) with no risk of the engine

Above: A Bf 109E-3 of III/JG2 Richthofen undergoing major engineering work which entails the complete removal of the Daimler Benz DB 601A engine.

attention on one enemy fighter for too long ran a serious risk of setting himself up for a surprise attack by another. On both sides, the really successful fighter pilots stalked their prey using the sun and/or cloud to remain unseen for as long as possible, and then announced their presence with an accurate burst that usually ended the encounter. Again contrary to the cliché image, chivalry had little place in such an action.

A textbook example of this type of combat occurred on the morning of 18 August when Oberleutnant Gerhard Schoepfel of III/JG 26 was leading a "Freijagd" over Kent. Below him he caught sight of a formation of Hurricanes of No 501 Squadron in the climb. Ordering his pilots to remain at altitude and cover should he need it, Schoepfel went down to engage the enemy alone. Unseen, he sneaked his Bf 109 in behind the formation and shot down four Hurricanes in rapid succession. He might have got more, but the Bf 109 was hit by debris from the last of its victims and Schoepfel was forced to break off the action. The incident demonstrates well the effectiveness of the Bf 109 in the hands of a talented pilot.

Top: A Bf 109E-4B/Trop of 10 (Jabo) JG27 is loaded with an SC250 (550lb) bomb at a forward landing ground in the Western Desert, North Africa, 1942.

Above: A newly-delivered Bf 109E-3 replacement aircraft for III/JG26 readied for painting in unit colours and with its DB601Aa engine out.

Combat

ESCORT DUTY

On 7 September the attack on England shifted to London itelf, a target at the limit of the Bf 109's effective combat radius of action from its airfields in the Pas de Calais area. During this phase of the battle the German fighter units engaged in three types of operation in support of bombers attacking the English capital: freijagd sweeps ahead of the raiding force to break up the enemy fighter units before they could get close to the bombers; intermediate escort by units that stayed with their allocated bomber formations until enemy fighters approached, but which were then free to break away and go into action; and close escort units with strict orders to

Above: A Bf 109E-4 of I/JG3 in its Battle of Britain markings in the autumn of 1940. The dragon insignia has been left in a box on the yellow nose.

remain with their allocated bombers no matter what the enemy did. The close escort operations were always unpopular, as Oberleutnant Hans Schmoller-Haldy of JG 54 explained: ''It gave the bomber crews the feeling they were being protected, and it might have deterred some of the enemy pilots. But for us fighter pilots it was very bad. We needed the advantages of altitude and speed so we could engage the enemy on favourable terms. As it was, the British had the initiative of when and how to attack.

''The Heinkel 111s cruised at approximately 13,000ft (4,000m) and about 190mph (300kmh). On close escort we flew at about 230mph (370kmh) weaving from side to side to keep station on them. We needed to maintain speed, otherwise the 109s would have taken too long to accelerate to fighting speed if we were bounced by Spitfires.

''We had to stay with the bombers until our formation came under attack. When we saw the British fighters approaching we would want to accelerate to engage them. But our commander would call 'Everybody stay with the bombers'. We handed to the enemy the initiative of when and how they would attack us. Until they did we had to stay close to the bombers or their people would complain and there would be recriminations later.''

Bf 109 UNITS DURING BATTLE OF BRITAIN, 7 SEPTEMBER 1940

First figure refers to aircraft total, second figure to the numbers serviceable.

Luftflotte 2 (Holland, Belgium, north-eastern France)			
Jagdgeschwader 1			
Stab	4	3	Pas de Calais area
Jagdgeschwader 3			
Stab	3	3	Samer
I Gruppe	23	14	Samer
II Gruppe	24	21	Samer
III Gruppe	25	23	Desvres
Jagdgeschwader 26			
Stab	4	3	Audembert
I Gruppe	27	20	Audembert
II Gruppe	32	28	Marquise
III Gruppe	29	26	Caffiers
Jagdgeschwader 27			
Stab	5	4	Etaples
I Gruppe	33	27	Etaples
II Gruppe	37	33	Montreuil
III Gruppe	31	27	Sempy
Jagdgeschwader 51			
Stab	5	4	Saint Omer
I Gruppe	36	33	Saint Omer, Saint Inglevert
II Gruppe	22	13	Saint Omer, Saint Inglevert
III Gruppe	44	31	Saint Omer
Jagdgeschwader 52			
Stab	2	1	Laon/Couvron
I Gruppe	21	17	Laon/Couvron
II Gruppe	28	23	Pas de Calais area
III Gruppe	31	16	Pas de Calais area

Jagdgeschwader 53			
Stab	2	2	Pas de Calais area
II Gruppe	33	24	Wissant
III Gruppe	30	22	Pas de Calais area
Jagdgeschwader 54			
Stab	4	2	Holland
I Gruppe	28	23	Holland
II Gruppe	35	27	Holland
III Gruppe	28	23	Holland
Jagdgeschwader 77			
I Gruppe	42	40	Pas de Calais area
Erprobungsgruppe 210			
	26	17	Denain (fighter-bomber unit, also operated Bf 110s)
Luftflotte 3 (north-western France)			
Jagdgeschwader 2			
Stab	5	2	Beaumont-le-Roger
I Gruppe	29	24	Beaumont-le-Roger
II Gruppe	22	18	Beaumont-le-Roger
III Gruppe	30	19	Le Havre
Jagdgeschwader 53			
I Gruppe	34	27	Brittany area
Lehr Geschwader 2			
II Gruppe	32	27	Saint Omer (fighter-bomber unit)
Luftflotte 5 (Norway)			
Jagdgeschwader 77			
II Gruppe	44	35	Southern Norway

Messerschmitt Bf 109

FIGHTER BOMBERS

During the early part of the Battle of Britain two units, II/Lehrgeschwader 2 and Erprobungsgruppe 210, operated Bf 109E-1s in the fighter-bomber role against targets in southern England and, later, against London itself. Some E-4 fighters then being built were modified with racks and re-designated E-4/B fighter bombers. During these missions the usual load carried by the Bf 109 was one SC 250 (550lb of high-explosive), or four SC 50s (110lb) or one Flamm 250 (550lb incendiary). As the large-scale actions of August and September petered out, more and more Bf 109s were employed in the fighter-bomber role. During attacks on London the fighter-bombers usually approached the target by "Ketten" of threes, from altitudes of above 20,000ft (6,000m). Over the city the leader banked his

Above: A rare shot of a Bf 109T-2 intended for carrier operations and fitted with folding wings, a strengthened undercarriage and an arrester hook.

aircraft to pick out the target; then, with his two wing-men in close formation on either side of him, he pushed his Messerschmitt into a 45deg dive and lined up on the target. After a descent through 3,000ft (900m) he released his bomb load, as did his

wing-men, and the three fighter-bombers pulled out of their dives.

Such high-altitude attacks did not make for accurate or effective bombing. But on the other hand the defending fighters found the German fighter-bombers difficult to engage and the latter suffered minimal losses. During the autumn of 1940 one Staffel in each Jagdgeschwader or Zerstoerergeschwader converted to the fighter-bomber role, and from the beginning of October the majority of daylight attacks on England were carried out by fighter-bombers. During the late Autumn even these attacks became less frequent, and by December they had petered out altogether. The Battle of Britain was over and the Luftwaffe had lost the crucial engagement.

THE TRAEGER

One further development of the Bf 109E needs to be mentioned at this stage: the Bf 109T ("T" for Traeger or aircraft carrier), a fully navalized version modified for deck landing operations. This aircraft was intended to operate from aircraft carrier *Graf Zeppelin*, the hull of which was launched in 1938. The Bf 109T was fitted with an arrester hook, catapult spools on the fuselage and a strengthened undercarriage; there was also provision for the wings to fold outboard of the wing cannon. During 1939 the Fieseler plant began building a batch of 60 T-1 aircraft, but before they were finished the work on fitting out the aircraft carrier was halted. The Bf 109Ts had their arrester hooks and catapult spools removed and they were completed as land-based fighter-bombers, entering service with I/JG 77 during the Spring of 1941.

The "Emil" served the Luftwaffe well and it remained in production until 1941, even after it began to be supplanted by the new and more effective "Friedrich".

Above: A Bf 109E-4 of I/JG1 based at De Kooy, The Netherlands, in early 1941 after the invasion of the Low Countries a year earlier when few Bf 109s were lost in action.

Above: A Bf 109E-4/B fighter bomber from III/SKG210 based at El Daba, Libya, in October 1942. The bomb is an SC 250; the white band denotes service in the Mediterranean theatre.

DEVELOPING THE BREED FURTHER

Shortly after war broke out the Messerschmitt company initiated a programme to clean up the aerodynamic shape of the Bf 109 and to strengthen the airframe in order to exploit the extra power offered by later versions of the DB 601 engine. The result of their endeavours was the Bf 109F, the "Friedrich". The most significant external recognition features of the new version were the more-rounded spinner and more-streamlined nose contours running back from there, the rounded wing tips, the partially retractable tail wheel and the cantilever tailplane without supporting struts. Other, less obvious features were the redesigned supercharger air intake, protruding further from the cowling to give an increased ram effect for the airflow, and more efficient underwing radiators.

Some of these improvements were tested during the summer of 1940 on modified "Emils", then on the V 22,

Above: Early-production Bf 109F-1s in manufacturer's markings. The aircraft first flew with JG2 and JG26 in 1941.

V 23 and V 24 aircraft which served as prototypes for the Bf 109F. The initial sub-types of the Bf 109F were powered by the Daimler Benz DB 601N fitted to later versions of the "Emil". The F-0 pre-production aircraft and F-1 production aircraft were both armed with one MG FF cannon firing through the propeller spinner and two MG 17 machine guns mounted on top of the engine.

During the service evaluation of the "Friedrich", three aircraft crashed for reasons that were not immediately evident. This led to a temporary order

PERFORMANCE TABLE

Bf 109F-2		Bf 109E-1
6,174lb (2,800kg)	**Normal take-off weight**	5,535lb (2,510kg)
Daimler Benz DB601N	**Powerplant**	Daimler Benz DB601A
1,200hp	**Power output**	1,175hp
373mph (600km/h)	**Maximum speed**	342mph (547km/h)
36,100ft (11,000m)	**Service ceiling**	34,450ft (10,500m)
546 miles (880km) with 66 Imp gal (300 litres) drop tank	**Range**	410 miles (660km)

Right, top: A Bf 109E-7/B of II/SchG1 operating on the Stalingrad Front in the winter of 1942-43. It carries the infantry assault badge emblem.

Right, centre: A Bf 109E-7B of the famed Wespen-Geschwader in 1941. The yellow engine, rear fuselage band and wingtips denote service on the Eastern Front.

Right, bottom: A Bf 109E-7 of III/JG26 Schlageter based at Gela, Sicily, during the spring of 1941. The red heart emblem belongs to 7 Staffel.

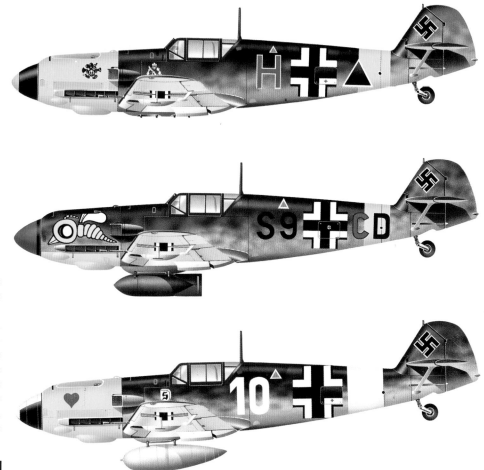

to ground the aircraft. During the detailed investigation that followed, the cause of the accidents was discovered: if the engine was run at critical rpm settings, it set up a sympathetic oscillation which caused a structural failure of the new cantilever tailplane. The addition of strengthening plates to the tailplane solved the problem, and once aircraft had received the modification the ''Friedrich'' was allowed to resume flying.

FORMIDABLE ''FRIEDRICH''

Only a few F-1s had been built before this sub-type was superseded in production by the F-2, which was fitted with an MG 151/15 cannon of 15mm calibre in place of the engine-mounted MG FF. A much more effective and faster-firing weapon than its predecessor, the MG 151/15 was belt fed from a 200-round magazine. For almost a year, the F-2 would remain the most important production sub-type of the Bf 109.

During the spring of 1941 the ''Friedrich'' entered service with Jagdgeschwader 2 and 26. Based in northern France, these fighter units were the most active in the Luftwaffe at that time, being responsible for countering the RAF attacks on targets on the fringes of occupied Europe. The arrival of the Bf 109F coincided with the deliveries of Mark V Spitfires to the RAF, thereby maintaining the qualitative balance between the two

Left: A fully operational Bf 109F-1 photographed outside a makeshift hangar in 1941 and wearing the markings of the kommandeur of III/JG2.

Developing the Breed Further

sides' fighter forces. By June of 1941 two-thirds of the Luftwaffe fighter force had converted to the F-2.

Meanwhile, fighter units equipped with Es had moved into bases in Rumania and Bulgaria in support of Balkan operations, many directed against Yugoslav E-3s bought in 1940. Other Es were tropicalized and transferred to North Africa.

GLORY DAYS IN RUSSIA

The large scale deployment of the Bf 109F and, later, the new Focke Wulf Fw 190 for the invasion of the USSR ensured that Luftwaffe fighter units operated aircraft that were in most cases superior to those of the enemy. The introduction of the F-3 and F-4 sub-types, which superseded the F-2 in

Left: Bf 109Fs of I/JG53 Pik As in desert camouflage in 1942. The type was quick to establish superiority over RAF fighters in the Western Desert theatre.

Above: A Bf 109F-4 of III/JG26 outside a camouflaged dispersal hangar in nothern France, 1942.

production at the end of 1941 and were fitted with the more powerful DB 601E engine, helped to maintain this qualitative advantage well into 1942.

These were great times for the German fighter pilots and the more talented ''Experten'' built up huge scores. There were plenty of opportunities for everyone, however, and even the inexperienced pilots could notch up victories. In the Summer of 1942 Walther Hagenah was posted to I/JG 3 in Russia straight from training. He operated the Bf 109F-4 flying as wing man to Oberfeldwebel Otto Wessling. Hagenah told this author: ''Wessling was a superb leader who seemed to be able to score hits from ranges as great as 1,300ft (400m). He would manoeuvre into a position of advantage above his enemy, dive on his prey and open fire from long range, hit his enemy and pull away without getting close to his foe.

''My first weeks as an operational fighter pilot were a disappointment. To

Above: A Bf 109F-2 of III/JG54 Grunherz in winter camouflage on the Leningrad Front, 1942-42. It

sports the gruppe emblem and the sinister red devil's head of the gruppe's 9 Staffeln.

Above: A Bf 109F-2/Trop of I/JG77 based at Comiso, Sicily, in the summer of 1942. Note the

white paint finish of the Mediterranean scheme on the nose, wingtips and rear fuselage.

be sure I fired at enemy aircraft, but all I seemed to hit was the air. I was beginning to get discouraged. One day Wessling took me to one side on the ground and said 'Now it is time for you to make your first kill!'

"On 12 August 1942 we were on patrol on the central Russian Front and he spotted a pair of LAGG-3 fighters. He took us round into an attacking position on their tails and down we went. We came out of the sun and achieved surprise. He hit one of them from about 1,300ft (400m) and down it went. Then he called me and said 'Now you go ahead and hit the other one!' But the second Russian pilot had a lot of pluck and he really threw his aircraft about the sky in an effort to shake us off his tail.

"Then Wessling joined in the dogfight, but at the same time telling

Below: A Bf 109E-4B over Russia in 1942. The plane carries the geschwader-adjutant's symbol plus the Lion of Aspern emblem, one of several used by JG54.

Above: A Bf 109F of III/JG53 Pik As operating from a forward airfield in the bitterly cold Leningrad sector during the winter of 1941-42.

Above: A Bf 109E-7 of JG5 with an early sand/dust filter fitted on the carburettor air intake on the port side of the engine.

me what I had to do to get 'my' kill. Eventually he succeeded in manoeuvring both me and the Russian fighter into a position where I could open fire at it — just as a gamekeeper will chase a deer into a position where a wealthy man can hit it with his gun. All I had to do was obey Wessling's instructions and fire when he said, and I hit the fighter. So I got my first kill. I was very proud. Wessling was big enough to keep quiet about how I got it."

Developing the Breed Further

WAR AND DEATH IN AFRICA

The foremost exponent of the "Friedrich" was Leutnant Hans Joachim Marseille. Credited with seven victories during the Battle of Britain, he arrived in North Africa early in 1941 and joined Jagdgeschwader 27. Initially, his victory total built up slowly, but from the beginning of 1942 it increased by leaps and bounds. There were few Spitfires in the area, and the Bf 109F-4/Trop possessed a clear superiority over the Hurricane and Tomahawk fighters operated by the RAF and its allies. During a remarkable action near Bir Hakeim on 3 June, Marseille shot down six Tomahawks of No 5 Squadron South African Air Force within a space of 11 minutes. All are confirmed in Allied records. A couple of weeks later Marseille's victory score passed the 100 mark and in September it reached 150 — he was the first fighter pilot ever to reach such a score. Marseille met his death on 30 September 1942, having been credited with 158 victories; as was often the case, the enemy played no part in the demise of the fighter ace. As he was returning from an uneventful bomber escort mission his engine caught fire. Escorted by his Staffel he stayed with the aircraft until he had regained German-held territory, but then his luck deserted him. As he jumped from the stricken Messerschmitt it appears that he struck the tail and was knocked unconscious. He never pulled the ripcord and his parachute pack was still unopened when he struck the ground.

INCREASED FIREPOWER

The close-mounted battery of one cannon and two machine guns gave the "Friedrich" a concentrated pattern of fire that proved highly effective against enemy fighters and light

Above: A Bf 109E-8 fitted experimentally with skis. The wheel wells are faired over and painted to look as if the normal undercarriage is extended.

bombers. Against four-engined bombers, however, it was to prove to be another matter altogether. They were reasonably armoured for protection and carried heavy defensive firepower.

From mid-1942 the Bf 109F units operating over western Europe and North Africa found themselves in increasingly frequent combat against American B-17s and B-24s. To knock down one of the big bombers required about 20 hits with 20mm explosive rounds. During a brief firing pass delivered through the defensive crossfire of a formation of heavy bombers, it was found that only the most capable "Experten" could achieve sufficient hits with a single cannon.

In answer to this problem a field modification kit was developed for the Bf 109F. A blister was built containing an MG 151/20 cannon with 120 rounds which could be mounted under each wing outboard of the propeller disc. The three-cannon armament nearly trebled the fire power of the standard "Friedrich", but the im-

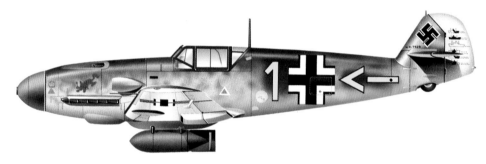

Above: A Bf 109F-4/B fighter bomber of 10 (Jabo)/JG2 Richthofen operating from coastal sites in France in 1942. Note the claimed tally of ships painted on the rudder.

Above: A Bf 109F-4/Trop from 6 Staffel of JG53 based at Comiso for the Luftwaffe's concerted assault on Malta. Note the sand/dust filter fitted on the carburettor air intake.

provement was bought at some cost to performance and general handling. It was the first indication of a problem that was to become progressively more serious for the Bf 109 and other German fighter types from now on: if they had sufficient firepower to engage the American heavy bombers successfully, the additional weight placed them in a poor position if they encountered Allied fighters.

That particular problem would not dog the ''Friedrich'' for long, for by the beginning of 1942 it was about to be superseded in production by another new variant of Willy Messerschmitt's little fighter.

BOOSTING THE ENGINE

During the Second World War, every fighter type that remained in production for any length of time underwent a continuous process of modification to improve its fighting capability. It would be fitted with more powerful (and invariably heavier) engines to boost performance, progressively more effective (and inevitably heavier) armaments, larger (and heavier) fuel tankage and more (and heavier) items of operational equipment. The airframe had to be

Above: A Bf 109E-4/Trop of I/JG27 demonstrates the effectiveness of its camouflage over the Libyan desert in 1941.

Below: A Bf 109F-4/Trop of III/JG53 Pik As uses ailerons during a taxi and raises a dust cloud on the rough strip.

Above: A reconnaissance fighter, the Bf 109F-6 from Sardinian-based Fernaufklaerungsgruppe 122. Armament is removed and cameras installed in the rear fuselage.

stiffened periodically in order to restore the aircraft to its original strength factor, thereby adding yet another twist to its spiralling weight.

No aircraft was afflicted more by that process than the Bf 109. It had led the field and even at the outbreak of the war it was already fairly well advanced along its development life.

Developing the Breed Further

Left, top: Bf 109E-7s from II/JG1, a unit that operated in the role of deence of the Reich for most of the war following the Battle of Britain.

Left, centre: A Bf 109G-10, with a clear-vision canopy, carrying the markings of the kommandeur of III Staffel of JG54.

Left, bottom: A Bf 109G-5 of 7/JG27 in late-1943 when this staffel was dispersed around the eastern Mediterranean acting as semi-independent schwarme.

With every increase in weight there was a proportionate increase in wing loading, which in turn gave rise to progressively higher landing speeds and deterioration in handling characteristics. In the opinion of many a German fighter pilot, the "Friedrich" represented the pinnacle of development of the Bf 109 as a fighting aircraft. After that it seemed that almost every change was for the worse.

During the late war period large numbers of Bf 109s, beginning with the E-7 and then the F-2, were fitted with the MW-50 or the GM-1 power-boosting systems, and a few aircraft carried both. The MW-50 system injected a mixture of water and methanol in equal parts into the supercharger, to improve engine performance at altitudes *below* the rated one. The methanol served as an antifreeze agent. The water did the work, serving as an anti-detonant, cooling the charge and enabling a higher compression ratio to be used. Injected at a rate of half a gallon (2.2 litres) per minute, MW-50 increased the power of the DB 605 by between 120 and 150hp for a maximum of ten minutes. The installation weighed about 300lb (135kg).

The GM-1 system injected nitrousoxide (laughing gas) into the super-

Above: A Bf 109G-6 belonging to III/JG53 pictured at a forward airfield in Sicily, 1943. This variant had two 0.8in (20mm) cannon fitted to the wing.

charger to improve performance at altitudes *above* the rated altitude of the engine. Stored as a liquid at minus-88deg (C) in heavily lagged containers, the nitrous-oxide provided additional oxygen for combustion, acted as an anti-detonant and cooled the charge. The effect was to maintain engine power at altitudes greater than was otherwise possible. The DB 605 DCM engine, for example, developed a maximum of 1,550hp at its rated altitude of 19,600ft (5,900m) (above this altitude the engine's output would otherwise decrease progressively). But with GM-1 injection at 16lb (7.2kg) per minute, the engine developed 1,350hp at 32,800ft (10,000m). With full nitrous oxide containers, the GM-1 installation weighed approximately 660lb (300kg).

THE "GUSTAV"

Ideally, the Bf 109 should have been phased out of production from mid-1942 in favour of a brand new type such as the Messerschmitt Me 209; but the latter was not yet ready to go into service (and it never would). In any case, at that time the war seemed to be going well for Germany and there was every reason to believe that the eastern campaign would conclude

successfully by the autumn.

As the High Command saw it, the re-tooling of factories to build a new type of fighter would inevitably lead to a drop in deliveries. On the other hand, a new version of the Bf 109, with a slightly more powerful engine and more armament, could be introduced without disrupting production. It seemed that this would provide a short term answer to the requirement. As so often happens in war, however, what starts as a short term palliative ends up as a long term and not very effective solution to the problem. The resultant version of the fighter, the Bf 109G or "Gustav", was, despite its flaws, built in far greater numbers than all the others of its breed put together.

The "Gustav" was designed around the new Daimler Benz 605 engine. Based on the DB 601, the DB 605 had a redesigned cylinder block which in-

Above: A Bf 109G-2 fitted with fuel tanks and a jettisonable extra wheel under the fuselage to provide ground clearance for an SC 500 bomb to be carried.

creased its capacity from 7.46Imp gal (33.9litres) to 7.85Imp gal (35.7litres) for no significant increase in the engine's external dimensions and provided an additional 175hp.

The initial production sub-type of the "Gustav", the G-1, was built in

Above: A Bf 109G-2 of II/JG54 Grunherz, based at Siverskaya, Russia, in the summer of 1942.

Note the unit's Vienna-Aspern coat of arms, and the horizontal bar which identifies II Gruppe.

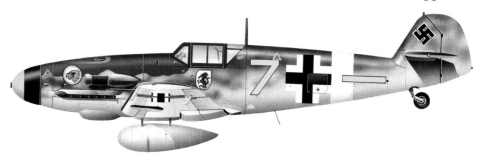

Above: A Bf 109G-2/Trop of II/JG51 Molders, based at Casa Zeppera, Sardinia, in the summer

of 1943. The gruppe motif below the cockpit carries the slogan "God Help England".

Developing the Breed Further

SPECIFICATION

Bf109 G-2

Dimensions
Length: 29ft 0½in (8.85m)
Wing span: 32ft 6½in (9.92m)
Gross wing area: 173sq ft (16.1m²)

Weights
Empty: 5,690lb (2,580kg)
Normal take-off: 6,836lb (3,100kg)

Power
1 x Daimler Benz DB605A liquid-cooled 12-cylinder inverted-Vee piston engine rated at 1,475hp, fitted with GM-1 nitrous- oxide injection to boost power above the rated altitude.

Performance
Maximum speed: 317mph (510km/h) at sea level, 397mph (640km/h) at 20,700ft (6,300m). With GM-1 injection, 406mph (654km/h) at 28,535ft (8,700m)
Initial rate of climb: 4,590ft/min (23m/sec)
Service ceiling: 39,360ft (12,000m)
Maximum range with 66 Imp gal (300litre) drop tank: 528 miles (850km)

small numbers. It featured the GM-1 power-boosting as well as a rudimentary pressurized cabin for the pilot. Initially, this version retained the one 20mm cannon and two 7.9mm machine gun armament of the F-4 sub-type. The G-2, the first sub-type of the "Gustav" to go into service, went into production at about the same time as the G-1 and was essentially similar but lacked cabin pressurization. The G-3 and G-4 were developments of the G-1 and G-2 respectively, but they carried the FuG 17 VHF radio in place of the FuG 7 HF radio. The G-5 was fitted with two MG 131 13mm machine guns on top of the engine in place of the MG 17s. From the G-5 onward, all subsequent fighter versions of the "Gustav" would carry MG 131s in the fuselage installation, giving rise to a pair of bulges in front of the cockpit which covered the breech mechanism.

During May 1942 a total of 234 Bf 109s came off the production lines at the three factories building the type — the Messerschmitt plant at Regensburg, the Erla plant at Leipzig and the WNF plant near Vienna. Most of the aircraft were "Gustavs", and they represented more than two-thirds of the single-engined fighters delivered to the Luftwaffe that month.

The next major production variant was the G-6, which started to come off the assembly lines during the Autumn of 1942. This sub-type was designed to accept several different versions of the DB 605 engine, with MW-50 or GM-1 power-boosting as required, and it could also accept a range of field modification kits by which the aircraft could be "customized" for specific operational roles. For example, the R-1

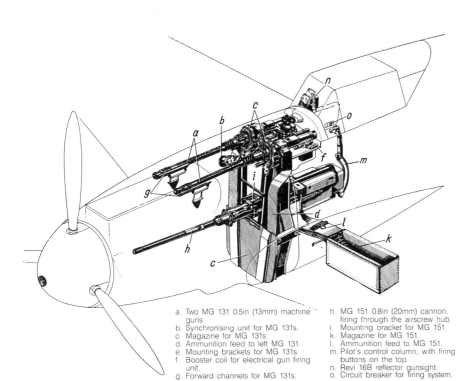

a. Two MG 131 0.5in (13mm) machine guns
b. Synchronising unit for MG 131s.
c. Magazine for MG 131s.
d. Ammunition feed to left MG 131.
e. Mounting brackets for MG 131s.
f. Booster coil for electrical gun firing unit.
g. Forward channels for MG 131s.

h. MG 151 0.8in (20mm) cannon, firing through the airscrew hub.
i. Mounting bracket for MG 151.
k. Magazine for MG 151.
l. Ammunition feed to MG 151.
m. Pilot's control column, with firing buttons on the top.
n. Revi 16B reflector gunsight.
o. Circuit breaker for firing system.

sudden and rapid deterioration in Germany's war fortunes. On one front after another she was thrown on to the defensive and the Luftwaffe found itself in need of more and more fighter aircraft. In 1943 production of the Bf 109 was doubled, and in the course of the year the three factories delivered 6,379 new aircraft — all of them "Gustavs". Added to these were a further 39 machines from the new Györ production line in Hungary.

DEFENCE OF THE REICH

Throughout 1943 there was a progressive increase in the strength and the frequency of daylight attacks by US heavy bombers on targets in Germany. What had started as infrequent raids by relatively small numbers of bombers against fringe targets grew inexorably into deep penetration attacks by several hundred bombers able to inflict considerable devastation. To

Above: The standard fuselage armament of the Bf 109G-5 and G-6 consisted of a 0.8in (20mm) MG 151 cannon firing through the airscrew hub, plus two 0.5in (13mm) MG 131 heavy machine guns above the engine cowling synchronized to fire through the aircraft's airscrew.

Right: A Bf 109G-2 of II/JG11 at Jever in late-1943 fitted with underwing launchers for WGR 210 Dodel rockets.

kit provided for the installation of a bomb rack under the fuselage to carry a bomb load of up to 550lb (250kg), and the R-2 installed a WGr 21 spin-stabilized unguided rocket and launcher under each wing for use against air or ground targets that acquired the name "Pulk-Zerstörer".

Coincident with the arrival of the G-6 into service in quantity came a

Developing the Breed Further

Top: Bf 109G-2s of 30 Jagddivision operating in the Wilde Sau single-engine night fighter role to try and counter the RAF's bomber attacks.

Above: A Bf 109G-6 bearing the markings of the kommandeur of I/JG27. It has a broad red band on the rear fuselage, used in 1944 for Reich air-defence units.

With or without rockets, the "Gustav" with its heavy gun armament and drop tank required careful handling, especially at low speeds. In the hands of an inexperienced pilot it could perform viciously, for if the throttle was opened too quickly during take-off, or if the fighter was lifted off the runway before it had reached full flying speed, it was liable to roll on its back and smash into the ground violently.

When they were waiting on the ground at readiness, the aircraft of II/JG 27 were drawn up by Staffeln in line abreast, the four Staffeln being dispersed evenly round the perimeter of the grass airfield. Once the scramble order was received it was important to get all the aircraft into the air and assembled into formation as rapidly as possible. To achieve this the Staffeln took off in pairs, moving on parallel headings separated by a few hundred yards and going in opposite directions. As the first two Staffeln passed the centre of the airfield, the other two Staffeln began their take-off runs also heading in opposite directions. Once the whole Gruppe was airborne, the leader would orbit over the base until it had assembled in formation and then climb away for his assigned patrol line.

The use of simultaneous take-offs by pairs of Staffeln provided the most rapid means of getting a Gruppe into the air and assembled in formation, but there was only a small margin for safety if anything went wrong. Seyringer recalled one particularly nerve-racking scramble when, due to incorrect fitting, some of the rockets were fired inadvertently from fighters in the Staffel taking off in the opposite direction. The missiles came scorching past the aircraft in Seyringer's Staffel just as they were getting airborne, causing considerable consternation but fortunately no damage!

Once the Gruppe had been vectored

meet the new threat, fighter units had to be pulled back from the fronts to help defend the homeland.

We may get an insight into the working of the German day fighter defences at this time from the impressions of Unteroffizier Hans Seyringer, who flew in the summer of 1943 with II/JG 27 based at Wiesbaden. The young pilot had come straight from

training with only 200 flying hours in his logbook. Seyringer's G-6 carried three 20mm cannon and two 13mm machine guns, and during interception missions a drop tank was usually carried. Some aircraft in the Gruppe carried the R-2 modification with a couple of 21cm rocket launchers under the wings, though Seyringer himself never flew with these weapons.

to within visual range of an enemy bomber formation, its commander would decide which type of attack to employ. Seyringer took part in a few head-on attacks, but he felt that the time spent manoeuvring into position for a head-on attack was out of all proportion to the very short firing pass which resulted. More often his Gruppe attacked the bombers from the rear, usually in four-aircraft "Schwarme" flying in line abreast or line astern. After the initial attack the "Schwarm" usually split into two pairs or "Rotten" for further firing runs.

For most of 1943 the American escort fighters were unable to penetrate far into Germany and II/JG 27 rarely encountered them. Seyringer thought that was just as well, for with its heavy armament he felt his "Gustav" was quite unsuitable for dog-fighting.

DESPERATE DAYS

At this time the German tactics to counter American heavy bombers were under continual development and units explored almost every possible method. Jagdgeschwader 1 even ex-

Above: A Bf 109G-6 of IV/JG5 which is painted in temporary snow-speckled camouflage for operations on the northern sector of the Eastern Front in the winter of 1943-44.

Above: A Bf 109G-6 of I/JG52 based in Romania during the summer of 1944. By this stage of the war the jagdgeschwader had 81 Bf 109s in its three gruppen, about 52 of them serviceable.

Below: Bf 109G-6s from III/JG27 lined-up at Wiesbaden-Erbenheim in 1944 in readiness for a scramble take-off to intercept raiding USAF bombers.

perimented with air-to-air bombing attacks, releasing time-fused 550lb (250kg) shells from Bf 109Gs flying above the bomber formation. The intention was to destroy the enemy planes, or damage them so they were forced to leave the protection of their formation and thereby became easy prey for other fighters. The problems of accurate aiming and getting the bombs to detonate at the correct altitude were never solved and most bombs exploded safely clear of their intended victims. Few enemy aircraft had been destroyed or damaged before this type of attack was abandoned. Also invented at this time was the nocturnal interception and pursuit technique named "Wilde Sau" or Wild Boar. A complete division of G-6s was formed to put it into action. It lasted, however, only until early 1944 whereupon it was disbanded.

From the spring of 1944 the American escort fighters were able to join

Developing the Breed Further

Above: This Bf 109G-6 landed in error at RAF Manston in July 1944 and was then put into RAF markings for flight tests against leading Allied fighters such as the Spitfire and Mustang.

with the bombers in flying to almost every part of Germany. The P-47s and P-51s were superior in performance to the defending Bf 109s, Fw 190s, Bf 110s and Me 410s, which were often outnumbered and took increasingly heavy losses. At the end of April, Generalmajor Adolf Galland had been moved to report to his superiors: "Between January and April 1944 our day fighter arm lost more than 1,000 pilots. They included our best Staffel, Gruppe and Geschwader commanders . . . The time has come when our force is within sight of collapse."

Now even the best of the German pilots had to fight for their survival, and one by one they were being picked off. Gone were the days when these "*Experten*" could afford to "play" enemy fighters and allow their less experienced colleagues to get easy kills, as had been the case over Russia a couple of years earlier. One of those who fell in combat with American fighters in April 1944 was Leutnant Otto Wessling, then credited with 83 victories, who had set up Walther Hagenah's first kill.

By this time the greater part of the Luftwaffe fighter force was committed to the defence of the homeland. The losses in pilots far outstripped the ability of the German training organization to provide replacements, and it was necessary to withdraw additional

Bf 109 FRONT LINE UNITS, 31 MAY 1944		

First figure refers to aircraft total, second figure to the numbers serviceable. Units marked with an asterisk operated other types in addition to the Bf 109. Nahaufklaerungsgruppen were tactical reconnaissance units.

Luftflotte Reich (Greater Germany)
Jagdgeschwader 1
  III Gruppe 48 21
Jagdgeschwader 3
  Stab 4 2
  I Gruppe 26 9
  II Gruppe 29 23
  III Gruppe 31 9
Jagdgeschwader 5
  I Gruppe 43 36
  II Gruppe 44 36
Jagdgeschwader 11
  Stab 4 3
  II Gruppe 31 14
Jagdgeschwader 27
  Stab 4 4
  I Gruppe 41 31
  II Gruppe 24 12 — Unit reforming
  III Gruppe 26 20
  IV Gruppe 18 12
Jagdgeschwader 53
  II Gruppe 31 14
Jagdgeschwader 300
  I Gruppe 29 19 — Day/Night fighter unit
  III Gruppe 27 25 — Day/Night fighter unit
Jagdgeschwader 301
  I Gruppe 25 21
Jagdgeschwader 302
  I Gruppe 27 11
Nachtjagdgruppe 10
  8 5 — *Night fighter unit
Einsatzstaffel JG 104
  4 4 — Training school, fighters flown on operations by instructors.
Einsatzstaffel JG 106
  5 3 — As above
Einsatzstaffel JG 108
  12 6 — As above
Nahaufklaerungsgruppen
  NAGr8 2 2 — Unit reforming
  NAGr14 2 0 — Unit reforming
Luftflotte 2 (central Mediterranean)
Jagdgeschwader 4
  I Gruppe 13 10
Jagdgeschwader 53
  III Gruppe 13 17

Jagdgeschwader 77
  Stab 4 3
  I Gruppe 21 10
  II Gruppe 54 41

Luftflotte 3 (France, Belgium, Holland)
Jagdgeschwader 2
  II Gruppe 13 11
Jagdgeschwader 26
  III Gruppe 37 21
Nahaufklaerungsgruppe
  NAGr13 42 24

Luftflotte 1 (Eastern Front)
Nahaufklaerungsgruppe
  NAGr5 30 24

Luftflotte 4 (Eastern Front)
Jagdgeschwader 51
  IV Gruppe 35 22
Jagdgeschwader 52
  Stab 1 1
  I Gruppe 31 10
  II Gruppe 23 18
  III Gruppe 26 23
Jagdgeschwader 53
  I Gruppe 33 30
Jagdgeschwader 77
  III Gruppe 31 24
Jagdgeschwader 301
  II Gruppe 11 10 — Part of unit

Luftflotte 5 (Eastern Front)
Jagdgeschwader 5
  III Gruppe 33 33
  IV Gruppe 33 30

Luftflotte 6 (Eastern Front)
Jagdgeschwader 51
  I Gruppe 44 34
  III Gruppe 40 32
Nahaufklaerungsgruppen
  NAGr4 24 9*
  NAGr10 11 4*

Luftwaffen Kommando Sudost (Balkans)
Jagdgeschwader 51
  II Gruppe 55 46
Jagdgeschwader 301
  II Gruppe 9 8
Nahaufklaerungsgruppe
  NAGr12 15 5

fighter Gruppen from the battle fronts. In the spring of 1944 the Allied strategic bombing forces had focused their attack on the German aircraft industry and several of the major airframe and engine plants were hit hard, but there was never any shortage of Bf 109s. To counter the Allied move the German aircraft industry underwent a large scale reorganization with the aim of stepping up fighter production and reducing the industry's vulnerability to air attack. To concentrate resources for the production of fighters, almost all non-fighter programmes were halted. At the same time, aircraft production was dispersed into a large number of small factories and workshops spread throughout the country; the latter were difficult for the Allies to find, and those destroyed represented only a small loss to the production programme. These moves had the desired

Above: The prototype of the operational trainer version, the Bf 109G-12, was built by fitting a rear seat and extended canopy onto a G-5 airframe; others were made from G-1s and G-6s.

effect and during the course of 1944 the production of Bf 109s was again doubled, with the factories delivering a total of 14,212 new aircraft.

One particularly weak feature of the Bf 109, compared with other fighters of the late war period, was the heavily framed canopy with steel armour protecting the pilot's head, which restricted his view to the sides and the rear. Since the ability to see the enemy first decided many an air combat, this represented a major deficiency. To overcome the problem, a redesigned canopy appeared in 1944 which had far less framing than the earlier type and a slab of laminated glass behind the pilot's head instead of the vision-restricting steel plate. Nicknamed the "Galland Hood", the new canopy was fitted to many late-model Bf 109Gs, notably the G-12.

To extend the operational life of the "Gustav", the later sub-types were optimized to perform specific combat roles. For example, many G-10s coming off the production lines were built specifically for high-altitude fighter-versus-fighter combat. These aircraft were fitted with the DB 605D engine with an enlarged supercharger and GM-1 power-boosting, and to reduce weight their armament comprised only

Above: A Bf 109G-10 of I/JG3 Udet of the Reich Air Defence in the winter of 1944-45. When fitted with the DB 605DC engine, the G-10 was the fastest of the G-series fighters in service.

Above: A Bf 109G-6 from the Royal Bulgarian Air Force's 6th Fighter Polk or Regiment in 1944. They were used to defend Sofia and the Ploesti oilfields but suffered heavy loss rates.

Developing the Breed Further

one 20mm cannon and two 13mm machine guns. These aircraft were assigned to Bf 109 units providing top-cover for bomber-destroyer Gruppen operating other types.

FINAL VARIANTS

Although the "Gustav" remained in full production until the end of the war, two further versions of the Bf 109 also entered service. The Bf 109H was a high-altitude fighter version based on the G-5 and using the latter's pressurized cockpit. Inserts into the wing on each side of the fuselage increased the span by 11ft 1½in (3.39m) to 43ft 6in (13.25m), and added 62ft² (5.7m²) to the wing area for improved handling at altitudes above 40,000ft (12,200m). The H-1 was a fighter-reconnaissance sub-type armed with one MG 151/20 and two MG 17s and with provision to carry a vertical

Above: A Bf 109G-14 of III/JG3 Udet late in the war when it was flying escort missions for Fw 190 Sturmbock attacks against formations of USAF bombers.

camera, usually an Rb 75/30, in the rear fuselage. Built in small numbers, the H-1 underwent a service evaluation in France early in 1944 but this version saw little operational use.

The final production version of the

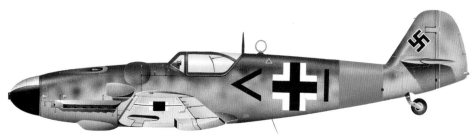

Above: A Bf 109G-14 of III/JG27 of the Reich Air Defence. The broad green tail band was introduced as this geschwader's identifier during the final doomed months of the war.

Above: A Bf 109G-14 of IV/JG53 Pik As, also serving with the Reich Air Defence by late 1944-45 and wearing its black fuselage band for geschwader identification purposes.

Bf 109 was the "K" or "Kurfurst", deliveries of which began in September 1944. Externally, the new fighter differed from the later sub-types of the "Gustav" in having a slightly higher engine cowling and slightly longer spinner, together with a distinctive fixed-trim tab projecting from the top of the rudder. It was also fitted with a re-designed tail wheel with a longer stroke leg and the so-called "Galland Hood" was standard on this version. The initial production sub-type, the K-2, had a pair of MG 151/15 15mm cannon mounted above the engine. The K-4 was similar to the K-2 but featured a pressurized cockpit. Intended as a bomber-destroyer, the K-6 was fitted with a Mk103 30mm high-velocity cannon firing through the airscrew spinner. This weapon was more than twice as heavy as the Mk108 30mm gun fitted to earlier versions of the fighter and this meant the unwieldy sub-type saw relatively little use. The final sub-type of the Bf 109 to go into production before the military collapse was the K-14, powered by the DB605L engine fitted with two-stage supercharging and with a maximum speed of 452mph (728kmh) at 19,700ft (6,000m).

There was also the abortive Bf 109 Zwilling project abandoned in 1944 after a prototype had been built. The idea was to marry two 109F airframes to produce a heavy "Zerstörer" but it was to come to nothing.

FIGHTING UNTIL THE END

In September 1944, Bf 109 production reached its all-time peak when 1,605 of these fighters were delivered to the Luftwaffe. Although the units operating the type were never short of aircraft, during the closing stages of the war fuel was much more difficult to come by. Leutnant Hans-Ulrich Flade, who flew Bf 109s with II/JG 27 early in 1945, recalled that if a fighter

Right: The unusual Mistel weapon consisted of a Bf 109F mounted atop a Ju 88 which had a warhead replacing its cabin. The Bf 109 pilot lined it up then detached.

Right, below: A Bf 109G-14 from III Gruppe taxies past repair work on the perimeter track at Merzhausen in 1944, a result of Allied bombing raids.

was damaged it was usually simpler to get a new one that repair the old: "We simply went to the depot nearby, where they had hundreds of brand-new 109s — G-10s, G-14s and even the very latest K models. There was no proper organization any more; the depot staff just said: 'There are the aircraft, take what you want and go away.' But getting fuel, that was more difficult . . ."

Flade's Gruppe had a strength of about 20 pilots and was losing two or three per day. Morale was low. "Each morning we pilots had breakfast together, and the replacements would come in. The older pilots regarded the young newcomers as though they had only days to live — and with reason, for the standard of fighter conversion training was now so low that most of the new pilots flew only two or three missions before they were shot down. I remember many conversations along these lines — not exactly a cheerful subject for a young man who had just joined his first operational unit!"

The Gruppe operated in the top-cover role, trying to keep the American escort fighters off the backs of other German fighters making for the bombers. He explained: "We followed the old rules: dive as a pair or a four out of the sun, make a quick attack to break up their formation and make them drop their tanks, then climb out of danger and assess the situation. If conditions were favourable, we would go down for a second attack. Always the escorts were so numerous that it would have been foolish to get into a dog-fight."

As Allied forces thrust progressively deeper into Germany, the aircraft factories and those building components and assemblies were overrun one by one. At the same time the general disruption of the transport system made it more difficult to get together components from the dispersed plants for final assembly. Despite these difficulties production of the Bf 109 continued to the very end of the war. During the last five months nearly 3,000 of these aircraft were delivered to the Luftwaffe, though many would remain on the ground for lack of fuel.

The Bf 109 was supplied to a number of foreign air forces from 1939 onward, most of the sales or transfers being to Germany's allies during the war. The recipients were all European, with the exception of the Japanese who did not take it into their inventory but took three E-4s to evaluate in 1941. A good number were also licence built abroad, principally in Hungary, Romania, Czechoslovakia and Spain.

The Swiss were the first to acquire it and by 1940 their Fliegertruppe had some 10 Jumo 210-engined Bf 109Cs and 80 DB601- and DB601A-engined E-1s and E-3s. These equipped six Fliegerkompagnien and were used to

Above: A Bf 109G-6 of the Swiss Fliegertruppe's Fliegerkompagnie 7. The aircraft was one of 12 sold in May 1944 in return for the neutral Swiss burning a Bf 110G-4B that had been captured.

Above: A Bf 109G-6 of the 3 Squadriglia of Italy's II Gruppo Caccia Terrestre based at Villafranca, Verona. Note the emblem of the Diavoli after whom the unit was nicknamed.

Above: A Bf 109E-3 of 6th Fighter Regiment of the Royal Yugoslav Air Force pictured prior to the German invasion of 1941. Markings were worn underwing.

engage Luftwaffe 109s which invaded Swiss air space during the war. The last Bf 109E, together with a small number of later acquired 109G-6s, was withdrawn from Fliegertruppe service in December 1949.

The Hungarians had ordered a number of Bf 109Es for delivery in 1940 but they were not handed over because of German sensitivity to the feelings of Romania who had not yet joined the Axis camp. Most bizarre was the shipment of five E-3s to the USSR under the terms of the Nazi-Soviet Pact, soon to be smashed asunder by the might of German Blitzkrieg. The Soviets acquired their 109s in exchange for raw materials the Germans needed to feed their war machine; similarly the Yugoslavs obtained some 70 Bf 109E-3s for a

Right: A Bf 109E-3 from a ground attack unit of the Royal Romanian Air Force. The vertical bars outside the cockpit signify the number of missions flown.

payment of metal ore in 1940. As with the Swiss, the Yugoslav 109s were pitted against 109s flown by the Luftwaffe when the Germans launched their attack on Yugoslavia in 1941.

As the Germans developed the Bf 109 further and marks were superseded by others, many of the "older" types were passed to those countries in Europe who had joined in the attack on the USSR. By 1941 Hungary was building the aircraft and continued to until 1944; in this way the Royal Hungarian Air Force received the Bf 109 in 1942, by which time they had a fighter squadron serving with the Germans on the Eastern Front. They later got the 109-G too, equipped another squadron for Russia, and were eventually to form nine squadrons for home defence. Similarly, the Italians converted two Gruppi to the 109F-4 and later 109Gs, as did the Spanish who formed a volunteer "foreign legion" with E-7s and F-4s which operated with JG27 and JG51 on the Eastern Front.

The Royal Romanian Air Corps obtained some 70 109E-4s which formed several fighter squadrons, and later got 109-Gs which were eventually used against the Germans following the Romanian coup in 1944. Meanwhile, the Bulgarians had absorbed nearly 20 109E-4s into one of their fighter regiments and later took delivery of well over 100 109Gs. Other nationalities formed 109-equipped volunteer units similar to Spain's Escuadron

Right: A Bf 109G-6 of the Aviazione della Repubblica Sociale Italiana undergoing undercarriage retraction tests in September 1944.

Above: Swiss Bf 109G-6, number J-701, one of a line-up of 12 Bf 109G-6s at Meiringen Air Base after their delivery from Germany to Dubendorf on 28 May 1944 to fulfill the agreed deal.

Azul, the Croatians having a unit fighting with JG52 in Russia and the Slovakians another.

The Finnish air arm also obtained the Bf 109 and they flew it very successfully against quality Soviet fighters. Indeed, the highest-scoring non-Germanic air ace was the Finn, Lentomestari Juutilainen, who obtained two-thirds of his 94 victories while flying "Gustavs" supplied to Finland in

Foreign and Post War Service

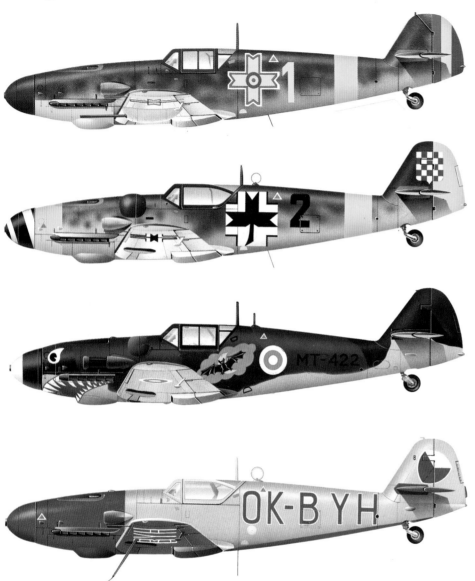

Left, from top to bottom: A Bf 109G-4/R6 of Corpul 1 Aerian of the Royal Romanian Air Force serving with I Fliegerkorps at Zhdanov in the Ukraine.

A Bf 109G-10/U4 from the Croatian Jagdstaffel based at Eichwald in November 1944 and operating under the command of Jagdfliegerfuhrer Ostpreussen.

A Bf 109G-5/U2 from the Finnish Ilmavoimien's HLeLv 31 based at Utti. This unit was commanded in the war by Eino Luukkanen, one of the top air aces.

A Bf 109G-14 or S.199 operating with the Czechoslovak National Air Guard in 1947. Note the omission of the distinctive engine cowl gun bulges.

own. The Bf 109G remained in Finnish service until 1954.

After the war, variants of the Bf 109 design were to continue in production in two countries. In Czechoslovakia the production lines set up by the Germans were brought back into operation and turned out a much-modified Bf 109G-14 powered by a Jumo 211 engine. Designated the S 199, the fighter entered service with the Czech Air Force in 1948. With the CS 199, a two-seat trainer version, some 550 of these aircraft were built. Twenty-five

1943. The Finns made excellent use of their 130-plus 109Gs and although they were debiliated by a lack of spare parts coming from Germany they managed to down over 250 Soviet aircraft for the loss of just 22 of their

Right: Czech Air Force Avia S.199s at Malacky in Slovakia in 1948. These aircraft were Czech manufactured Bf 109Gs fitted with Jumo 211 engines.

Above: A Bf 109F-4 of the Ungarische Jagdstaffel 1/I Vadasz Ezred operating under Luftwaffe command in the Stalingrad area during late 1942-43.

S199s were purchased by the fledgling state of Israel for its new air force and these saw action during the first Arab-Israeli war.

Meanwhile, assembly had begun at Hispano Aviation in Spain of a batch of twenty-five Bf 109G-2 airframes bought from Germany during the war. The deteriorating war situation prevented the Germans from supplying the DB 605s, so the aircraft were flown with Hispano Suiza HS 12Z engines and designated as HA-1109s. Hispano set up a production line to build a further 200 of these aircraft from scratch, some of them two-seaters which were designated the HA-1110. The work continued at a slow pace, however, and deliveries did not begin until 1952. In the following year the decision was taken to modify the aircraft to take the Rolls-Royce Merlin engine, and this gave a significant improvement in performance. As a result all HA-1109s and HA-1110s in service with the Spanish Air Force were fitted with the Merlin, being redesignated the HA-1112 M1L and the HA-1112-M4L respectively. A few examples would remain in service until 1967, more than 30 years after the Messerschmitt Bf 109 prototypes had first flown over that country.

Above: Finnish Air Force pilots and their Bf 109G-2s which entered service in March 1943 with Lentorykmentii 3. The G-6 replaced them in 1944 and remained until 1954.

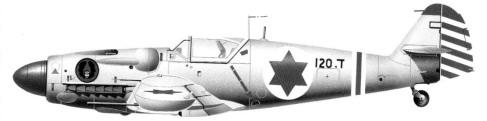

Above: Czech-built S.199 sold to the new Israeli Chel Ha'avir in 1948 and operated by No 101 Squadron, based at Herzaleah, who wore the death's head motif and the Star of David markings.

Above: Hispano Aviacion HA-1109-J11, a Bf 109G-2 fitted with the Hispano HS 12Z 89 engine, was first flown in 1947 but proved unsatisfactory in service with Spain's air force.

INDEX

Page numbers in **bold** type refer to subjects mentioned in captions to illustrations.

A

A variant 7
Armament **12**, **13**, **15**, 26, 30-31, 35

B

B (''Berta'') variants 7-11
line-up at Bayerische Flugzeugwerke **8**
prototype 7, **7**
production aircraft B-1 8
specification 9
transferred to Spain **10**, **13**, 14
wing form **8**
of Condor Legion **9**, **10**
Battle of Britain 20-25
Blitzkrieg 1940 19-20
Bombs
Flamm250 25
SC50 25
SC250 25, **25**
Bulgarian 109s **39**, 43

C

C variants 12
C-2 **12**
Camouflage **16**, **27**, 37
Canopy **39**, 40
Cockpit, 109E, **19**
Condor Legion 8-14, **9**
109s passed on to Spanish Air Force **13**, 14
Czech-built 109s (S.199) 44-45, **44**, **45**

D

D (''Dora'') variants 12, **13**, **15**
Defence of the Reich 35-39
Defiants (RAF) *versus* 109s 21
Design, original 7
Dunkirk 19

E

E (''Emil'') variants 14-15, **21**
cockpit **19**
E-1 **14**, **15**, **16**, **17**

performance 26
shoots down RAF bombers 17
E-3 **11**, **20**, **22**, **23**
specification 20
E-4 **24**, **25**
cutaway drawing **18-19**
E-4/Trop **31**
E-4B **25**, **29**
E-4B/Trop **23**
E-7 **29**, **32**
E-8 **30**
Engines
DB601 **14**, 22, **23**
DB605 33, **39**
Hispano Suiza 45
Jumo211 44, **44**
power-boosting systems 32-33
RR Kestrel 6
RR Merlin 45
Escort duty 24
Escort fighters, American 37-38
Exports 42-44

F

F (''Friedrich'') variants **14**, 26-31, **29**
increased firepower 30-31
attached on a Ju-88 **41**
prototypes 26
crashes during evaluation 26-27
F-1 **26**, **27**
F-2 **28**
performance 26
F-2/Trop **28**
F-3, F-4 28
F-4/Trop 30, **30**, **31**
F-4B **30**
F-6 **31**
Fighter-bomber versions 25, **25**
Finland's 109s 43-44, **44**, **45**
Focke Wulf
Fw159 6
Fw190 28
Formations (tactics) 11, 25, 37
Freijagd 21, 23

G

G (''Gustav'') variants 33-35
specification 34
unsuitability for dog-fighting 37
G-2 **33**, 36

G-2/Trop **33**
G-5 **32**, 35
G-6 **33**, **35**, **36**, **37**, **38**
G-6/R2 35
G-10 **32**, **39**
G-12 prototype **39**
G-14 **40**, **41**
Galland, Adolf 38
Galland Hood **39**, 40
GM-1 power-boosting system 32-33, **34**

H

H variants 40
Heinkel He112 6-7
Hispano Aviation 109s (HA1109-HA1112) 45, **45**
Hungary
builds 109s 43
Hungarian F-4 on Eastern Front **45**
Hurricanes (RAF) *versus* 109s 20-21
comparative performance 22-23, 30

I

Instrument panel, 109E, **19**
Israel's S.199s 45, **45**
Italy's 109s, **42**, 43

J

Japan evaluates 109 42
Ju-87 Stukas 20-1
Juutilainen, L., 43-44

K

K variants 40
Ketten 11, 25, 37

L

Luftwaffe strengths
September 1938 13
September 1939 14-16
May 1940 19
September 1940 24
May 1944 38
Luftwaffe Units
J88 8-14, **9**, **10**
JD30 36
JG-1 **15**, **25**, **32**, 37
JG-2 Richthofen **11**, 22, **26**, 27, **30**
JG-3 Udet **20**, 24, **39**, **40**
JG-5 **29**, 37
JG-11 35

JG-20 **14**
JG-26 Schlageter **12**, **15**, 17, **23**, **26**, 27
JG-27 **16**, **21**, **31**, **32**, 36-37, **36**, **37**, 40-41, **40**
Spanish contingent 43
JG-51 Molders **17**, 20-21, **33**
Spanish contingent 43
JG-52 37
Yugoslav contingent 43
JG-53 Pik As **17**, **29**, **30**, **31**, **33**, **40**
JG-54 Grunherz **29**, **32**, 33
JG-77 17, 25, **28**
in 1940 22
JG-102 12
JG-132 Richthofen 8, **11**, 15
JG-152 13
LG2, August 1940 22
SKG 210 **25**
ZG-1 17
Luukkanen, Eino **44**

M

Maiden flight 6
Marseille, Lt Hans Joachim 30
Messerschmitt, Willy 7, 13
Messerschmitt AG formed 13
MG17 12, 14, **15**, **17**, 26
MG131 35
MG151 27, **35**
MG FF 26
Moelders, Oberlt. Werner 11

O

Oerlikon FF cannon **13**
Offensive in the West, 1940 19-20

P

Performance, comparative 22-23
Poland 1939 15-16
Power-boosting systems 32-33
Production
peak 40
post-war 44-5
Prototypes
V1 6, **6**, **7**
V2, V3 7
V4 7, **7**
V13 11

V14 14
V22, V23, V24 26
V-23 **14**

R

Rocket launchers 35
Romania's 109s 43, **43**, 44
Rotten, 11, 37
RAF Squadrons
56 20-1
501 23
Russian Front 28-29, **28**, **29**

S

S.199 version 44-45, **44**
Schwarme 11, **11**, 37
Score record 30
Service trials
initial 6
F variant 26-27
Spain
builds 109s (HA-1109, -1110, -1112) 45, **45**
Eastern Front unit 43
Condor Legion, 8-14, 109B of 2/J88 **9**
109s passed to Spanish Air Force **13**, 14
Spitfire
performance *versus* 109 22-3
Mk.V 26
Swiss 109s 11, **11**, **42**, **42**, **43**

T

T variants 25, **25**
Tactics 11, 22-23, 36-37
Tomahawk's performance *versus* 109, 30
Tupolev Tu SB-2 10

U

USSR
acquires 109s 42

W

Wilde Sau technique 37
World record 11

Y

Yugoslav 109s 42-43, **44**

Z

Zwilling project 40